USA TODAY'S DEBATE: **VOICES AND PERSPECTIVES**

IMMIGRATION

Rich Diversity or Social Burden?

Robert Morrow

Twenty-First Century Books · Minneapolis

Twenty-First Century Books
A division of Lerner Publishing Group, Inc.
241 First Avenue North
Minneapolis, MN 55401 U.S.A.

Website address: www.lernerbooks.com

The publisher wishes to thank Ben Nussbaum and Phil Pruitt of USA TODAY for their help in preparing this book.

Library of Congress Cataloging-in-Publication Data

Morrow, Robert.
    Immigration : rich diversity or social burden? / by Robert Morrow.
        p.   cm. — (USA TODAY's debate voices and perspectives)
    Includes bibliographical references and index.
    ISBN 978-0-7613-4080-5 (lib. bdg. : alk. paper)
    1. United States—Emigration and immigration. 2. Immigrants—United States. I. Title.
JV6450.M6669 2010
325.73—dc22   2008049354

Manufactured in the United States of America
1 2 3 4 5 6 – DP – 15 14 13 12 11 10

CONTENTS

INTRODUCTION
The Immigration
Debate 5

CHAPTER ONE
The Story of
U.S. Immigration 13

CHAPTER TWO
Modern U.S.
Immigration Policy 41

CHAPTER THREE
A Country Divided 63

CHAPTER FOUR
Fences, Raids, and
Harsh Measures 81

CHAPTER FIVE
Immigrants and
the U.S. Economy 103

CHAPTER SIX
Culture and Morals . . . 117

Timeline 134
Glossary 137
Source Notes 139
Selected Bibliography 146
Organizations to Contact 147
Further Information 151
Index 156

INTRODUCTION

The Immigration Debate

MANY THINGS ARE UNIQUELY AMERICAN, SUCH as Disneyland, the Super Bowl, and iPods. But what makes the United States itself unique? It's the amazing blend of colors and cultures that make up the American people. Everyone who lives here is an immigrant or a descendant of immigrants. (An immigrant is a person who moves to make a home in a new country.) Even Native Americans, who lived here long before the first Europeans arrived, can be viewed as descendants of immigrants. Their ancestors were nomads (people who move their home base according to the season) from eastern Asia who made their way to western North America thousands of years ago.

The early history of the United States is a story of growth. After the Spanish and French explored North America in the 1500s, many Europeans began moving there to set up permanent colonies (dependent

Left: People of many cultures interact daily in U.S. schools, churches, businesses, and communities. Most people living in the United States are immigrants or descendants of immigrants.

territories). In 1620 the ship *Mayflower* arrived at Plymouth (in modern Massachusetts). It carried a group of British immigrants called Pilgrims, who were fleeing religious persecution in Great Britain. Many other European immigrants followed the Pilgrims. These early settlers built thirteen British colonies along the Atlantic coast of North America. Eventually they fought the Revolutionary War (1775–1783) with Great Britain (their colonial ruler), declared independence in 1776, and founded the United States of America.

Soon more people came to make a home in the new nation. Over the years, they built cities, factories, and railroads. Eventually the United States stretched from the Atlantic Ocean to the Pacific Ocean and became the wealthiest, most powerful nation on Earth. People called the United States a melting pot because a vast array of races, cultures, and ethnic groups had helped build it.

On the surface, the U.S. history of immigration may seem peaceful and orderly. But in reality, it has been rough and rocky.

Above: English Pilgrims aboard the *Mayflower* approach the shores of North America in the early 1600s. Native Americans had been living in the Americas for centuries by this time.

Sometimes the melting pot boils over.

Americans have not always welcomed new immigrants. In fact, Founding Father Benjamin Franklin, a close descendant of English immigrants, was angry about German settlers intruding into Pennsylvania, where he lived. Many of these settlers came from a region in Europe called the Rhenish Palatinate. Franklin asked, "Why should the Palatine Boors [rude, insensitive people] be suffered to swarm into our Settlements, and by herding together, establish their Language and Manners to the Exclusion of ours? Why should Pennsylvania, founded by the English, become a Colony of Aliens?"

Although many Americans did not and do not share Franklin's prejudice, others throughout history have argued that new immigrants cling too much to their old languages and customs, refusing to "Americanize." These Americans believe cultural diversity threatens our ability to live and act as one nation.

Americanization is only one of many issues that make up the immigration dilemma. The national debate over immigration also involves economic, moral, and social issues. Illegal immigration is a topic of especially heated debate. Illegal, or undocumented, immigrants are people who enter the United States without the permission of U.S. Citizenship and Immigration Services (USCIS), an arm of the U.S. Department of Homeland Security (DHS). (USCIS controls the flow of immigrants into the country.) In the early twenty-first century, illegal immigrants living in the United States number around twelve million people.

About one million immigrants—both legal and illegal—entered the United States in 2008 alone. The U.S. Census Bureau projects that the annual immigration rate will reach two million by 2050. This influx of newcomers has angered many Americans. Americans face a shortage of jobs. The nation's economy is unstable and its crime rate high. Many citizens

Above: On April 3, 2009, Jiverly Wong killed thirteen people and himself at an immigrant aid center in Binghamton, New York. This tragedy sparked new discussions about the effect of U.S. economic troubles on immigrants and vice versa.

believe that the United States doesn't need and cannot afford to accept any more people from foreign countries. They say that immigrants, especially illegal immigrants from Mexico and Central America, have swelled the ranks of welfare recipients and strained the nation's fragile economy. They argue that immigrants take jobs from deserving Americans. They also believe crime flourishes where many immigrants—especially illegal immigrants—live.

Some politicians, such as former governor Pete Wilson of California, have called for drastically reducing legal immigration. They also want harsh measures to discourage illegal immigration. For example, they would deny illegal immigrants basic medical care and public schooling and would require every U.S. citizen to carry a national identity card. Some immigration opponents want to repeal the Fourteenth Amendment to the U.S. Constitution, which guarantees citizenship to anyone born in the United States, regardless of their parents' legal status.

Fourteenth Amendment to the U.S. Constitution

The Fourteenth Amendment to the U.S. Constitution passed into law on July 9, 1868. The first paragraph of this amendment clarifies the definition of U.S. citizenship:

Section 1. All persons born or naturalized [granted citizenship] in the United States and subject to the jurisdiction [laws] thereof, are citizens of the United States and of the State wherein they reside. No State shall make or enforce any law which shall abridge [limit] the privileges or immunities [protections] of citizens of the United States; nor shall any State deprive any person of life, liberty, or property, without due process of law; nor deny to any person within its jurisdiction equal protection of the laws.

Many other U.S. citizens support immigration. They see the United States' immigrant heritage as the country's very foundation. They see that immigrant communities have revitalized U.S. neighborhoods, enriched the artistic and cultural fabric of society, and contributed badly needed service workers to the economy.

Senator Ted Kennedy of Massachusetts is one of these citizens. Speaking to the U.S. Senate in 2007 on the need for new national immigration laws, he said, "Our strength, our diversity, our innovation, our music, our hard work, our love of country, our dedication to family, faith and community— these are the fruits of our immigrant heritage and the source of our national strength. They have made America the envy of the world."

Economist Michael Mandel supports a wide-open immigration policy. In 2006 he wrote in *BusinessWeek* magazine,

"Immigration policy should facilitate the movement of people, just as trade policy facilitates the movement of goods. From an economic perspective, this is a no-brainer." He believes open borders would provide a clear benefit to both the U.S. and global economies. He finds little evidence to show that immigrants drive down wages or drain public funds.

In fact, many Americans see immigration as the key to the future of the United States. In a special issue called "America's Immigrant Challenge," the editors of *Time* magazine wrote in 1993, "There is no turning back: diversity breeds diversity. It is the fuel that runs today's America and, in a world being transformed daily by technologies that render distances meaningless, it puts America in the forefront of a new international order."

A bronze plaque inside the pedestal of the Statue of Liberty in New York Harbor displays *The New Colossus*, a sonnet by Emma Lazarus. It reads, in part:

> Here at our sea-washed, sunset gates shall stand
> A mighty woman with a torch, whose flame
> Is the imprisoned lightning, and her name
> Mother of Exiles. From her beacon-hand
> Glows world-wide welcome, her mild eyes command
> The air-bridged harbor that twin-cities frame.
> "Keep ancient lands, your storied pomp!" cries she
> With silent lips. "Give me your tired, your poor,
> Your huddled masses yearning to breathe free,
> The wretched refuse of your teeming shore;
> Send these, the homeless, tempest-tost to me,
> I lift my lamp beside the golden door!"

This famous poem describes one of the nation's highest goals—to welcome all people to its shores. Yet immigration has remained a thorny issue over the years. The debate does not represent a single

> " **Give me your tired, your poor /
> Your huddled masses yearning to
> breathe free. . . .** "

—EMMA LAZARUS, *THE NEW COLOSSUS*
INSCRIBED ON THE STATUE OF LIBERTY, 1883

issue with a single solution. Rather, it is a complex issue with many—sometimes overlapping—components. To fully understand U.S. attitudes toward immigration requires reviewing the history of immigration and immigration policy. It also involves investigating how immigration benefits and harms the American experience. And it means sampling public opinion and studying the causes and effects of illegal immigration. Examining these complexities can lead to a well-informed opinion about immigration in the United States.

Above: The inscription on a plaque inside the Statue of Liberty in New York offers immigrants a warm welcome to the United States.

CHAPTER ONE

The Story of U.S. Immigration

WHY HAVE PEOPLE IMMIGRATED TO THE UNITED States? If you could ask all the immigrants throughout U.S. history, you would probably get four basic answers:

- They wanted to immigrate because the United States offered a chance for personal improvement or economic gain.
- War, famine, poverty, or religious or political persecution drove them from their homelands.
- They wanted to reunite with family.
- They were forced to come here as slaves.

But what of the very first immigrants? Why did they come to a vast, unpopulated continent thousands of years ago?

THE FIRST ARRIVALS

Anthropologists (scientists who study the history of humans) say that the ancestors of Native Americans

Left: Crowds of people of different heritages and ethnicities walk down a street in New York City. The United States represents the promise of a better life for people from around the world.

arrived in North America during the last ice age, sometime between 30,000 and 12,000 B.C. They followed the Bering land bridge, which then connected Siberia to Alaska. These peoples were nomads seeking animals for food and fur.

Eventually the ice age ended, sea levels rose, and water covered the land bridge. By then North America's first immigrants were well established. They spread across North and South America. They built farms, villages, towns, and cities, including a trade center of forty thousand people near modern Saint Louis, Missouri.

By 1492, when Christopher Columbus came to the Americas from Europe, the region was home to about twenty million people. They practiced many religions and customs and spoke about nine hundred different languages. About one million Native Americans from two thousand nations occupied the land that would become the United States.

EUROPEAN EXPLORATION

Following Columbus, European explorers flocked to the

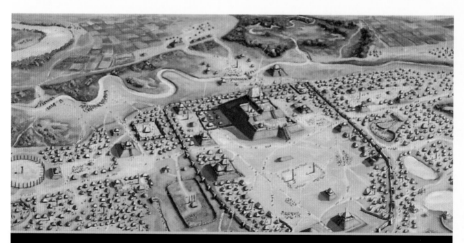

Above: Long before Europeans came to the Americas, Native American communities were thriving. This Cahokia village near modern-day Saint Louis, Missouri, was inhabited from about A.D. 700 to 1400.

Americas to seek fortune and establish colonies. In the 1500s, the Spanish founded numerous settlements and cities in South, Central, and North America. The Spanish built a colony near modern Saint Augustine, Florida, in 1513. In search of gold, a Spanish expedition traveled throughout the South (modern Georgia, South Carolina, North Carolina, Tennessee, Alabama, Arkansas, and Louisiana). The Spanish then conquered much of Mexico and the American Southwest. Spanish settlers established the city of San Diego (in modern California) in 1542 and the city of Santa Fe (in modern New Mexico) about sixty years later.

French fur traders also explored North America. From the Atlantic mouth of the Saint Lawrence River (in modern Canada), they traveled upstream. They founded the city of Quebec (also in modern Canada) in 1608. The French continued their exploration westward through the Great Lakes region. In 1682 French explorers traveled down the Mississippi River from the Great Lakes. They established several French-Indian trading centers along the river, including the cities of Saint Louis (in modern Missouri) and New Orleans (in modern Louisiana).

COLONIAL AMERICA

While the Spanish and French were exploring the interior and western regions of North America, the English were building thirteen colonies along the Atlantic coast. Many Americans trace their cultural heritage to these colonies.

Most of the early colonists were English citizens seeking either riches or religious freedom. In the late 1600s, fewer than two hundred thousand people were living in colonial America. Among the first arrivals during this time were black slaves and both black and white indentured servants. An indentured servant signed a contract to work without wages for a specified period of time (usually four to seven years). In exchange, the master paid for the servant's transportation, food, drink, clothing, lodging, and other necessities. Forced immigration

Above: Not all immigrants to the Americas came by choice. This print, published in *Harper's Weekly* in 1860, shows African slaves crowded aboard a ship sailing to the United States.

(slave trading) began in the early 1600s and continued for more than two centuries. During that period, slave traders shipped more than a half million Africans to the Americas and sold them into bondage.

Between 1700 and 1775, fewer English immigrants were coming to the Americas. But many more came from Scotland and Wales, as well as from Germany, Ireland, Sweden, Finland, the Netherlands, and France. The newcomers spread throughout colonial America. The Irish tended to settle in large northern cities.

The Welsh and Germans went to Pennsylvania and the Carolinas, the Swedes and Finns to Delaware, and the Dutch to New York. The French settled in South Carolina and most major New England towns. Sephardic Jews (descendants of Jews expelled from Spain and Portugal in the 1400s) settled in Rhode Island. By 1776 about 2.5 million people lived in the Americas, including half a million slaves.

AMERICAN INDEPENDENCE

In 1776 colonial America was still under British rule. Simply talking about independence was a crime of treason (trying to overthrow the government) punishable by hanging. Nevertheless, John Dunlap, an Irish immigrant in Philadelphia, Pennsylvania, risked his neck to print the first copies of the Declaration of Independence that year. This document declared the American colonies to be free from British rule.

On July 4, 1776, the Continental Congress met in Philadelphia and approved the Declaration of Independence. That night Dunlap worked by candlelight to print two hundred copies of the document. Dunlap was twenty-nine years old at the time. A few months later, during the Revolutionary War, he served with George Washington as an officer at the battles of Trenton and Princeton in New Jersey.

The story of the young Irishman Dunlap suggests that newcomers to colonial America wove immediately into the fabric of society. That was actually not the case. Established colonists did not always welcome new immigrants. For example, Protestant residents of some areas of New England discouraged Roman Catholics from settling

Above: This copy of the U.S. Declaration of Independence is one of the twenty-five surviving original prints produced by Irish immigrant John Dunlap in 1776.

there. Established Americans often complained about new, foreign-speaking, foreign-acting settlers.

Still, admiration of American diversity was common. For example, in 1782 French immigrant Michel-Guillaume-Jean de Crèvecoeur wrote of the American colonists:

> What then is the American, this new man? He is either [a] European, or the descendant of a European, hence that strange mixture of blood, which you will find in no other country. I could point out to you a family whose grandfather was an Englishman, whose wife was Dutch, whose son married a French woman, and whose present four sons now have four wives of different nations.... Here individuals of all nations are melted into a new race of men, whose labours and posterity [descendants] will one day cause great changes in the world.

" Here individuals of all nations are melted into a new race of men, whose labours and posterity will one day cause great changes in the world. "

—FRENCH IMMIGRANT MICHEL-GUILLAUME-JEAN DE CRÈVECOEUR
DESCRIBING THE NEW UNITED STATES OF AMERICA, 1782

IMMIGRATION SLOWS TO A TRICKLE

For about thirty years after the American Revolution ended in 1783, immigration to the United States slowed dramatically. Only 250,000 people arrived during that period. Great Britain had lost the Revolutionary War and had begun to discourage emigration (leaving one country to live in another). Wars in Europe and the United States also slowed immigration. Traveling by ship across the Atlantic Ocean was hazardous in wartime.

Despite the immigration slowdown, an important event happened during this time. This event, the Louisiana Purchase, strongly influenced later immigration. In 1803 the United States bought about 828,000 square miles (2.1 million square kilometers) of land from France for about fifteen million dollars. The land stretched from the Mississippi River west to the Rocky Mountains and from the Gulf of Mexico north to the 49th parallel (the modern border of Canada). Fifteen U.S. states and three Canadian provinces later formed—in whole or in part—from this territory.

A GREAT WAVE OF IMMIGRANTS

The U.S. government encouraged exploration and settlement across the Louisiana Purchase. For example, the government offered free or cheap land there. Such terms attracted Americans from the East Coast as well as European immigrants looking for a better life. So did famine and poverty in Ireland and

Above: The 1803 Louisiana Purchase, which extended as far west as the Rocky Mountains, nearly doubled the size of the United States. Thousands of people, including immigrants, would make the journey west to fill this new territory.

USA TODAY Snapshots®

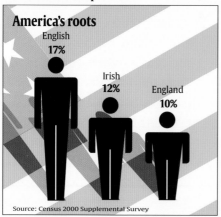

America's roots

English
17%

Irish
12%

England
10%

Source: Census 2000 Supplemental Survey

By USA TODAY, 2001

an old fortress on the southwestern tip of Manhattan Island. Then the U.S. Congress passed the Immigration Act of 1882, making immigration a federal concern. Castle Garden became a federal processing center. More than eight million immigrants entered the United States through this center.

Historians call members of the first great wave of immigrants to the independent United States "old immigrants." Old immigrants arrived during a time when the nation's doors were open to anyone who could buy a boat ticket or walk across the border. As George Washington had proclaimed at the end of the American Revolution, "The bosom of America is open . . . to the oppressed and persecuted of all Nations and Religions." Washington's words were eloquent, and millions of immigrants heeded them. But in reality, the United States did not offer these immigrants a warm welcome.

political upheaval in Germany. Altogether, roughly five million European immigrants came to the United States during the 1800s. This wave of immigration more than doubled the total immigrant population.

In the early 1800s, the U.S. government did not regulate immigration. Immigration was the business of individual states, many of which didn't have formal procedures or keep records. Immigrants typically got off their ships and simply became Americans. The process changed when immigration surged.

In 1855 the state of New York began processing all its immigrants at Castle Garden,

IRISH IMMIGRANTS

Among the old immigrants of the nineteenth century were the Irish. In the early 1800s, Ireland was home to eight million people. It was the most densely populated country in Europe. Most Irish peasants lived in poverty on small farms. They paid high rents for tiny plots and typically survived on potatoes. Potatoes were the only crop a small farm could grow in enough quantity to feed a family.

Between 1845 and 1847, poverty worsened in Ireland when potato crops failed due to a disease called potato blight. Crop failures caused widespread famine. Between 1846 and 1851, nearly one million Irish died of starvation and disease.

The potato famine and poverty in Ireland drove many Irish to the United States. During the two decades before 1860, 1.7 million Irish immigrants arrived. By 1870 the United States was home to 4.7 million Irish.

Although the United States offered free or cheap farmland, most Irish immigrants stayed on the eastern seaboard. Irish immigrants typically had little or no money to travel any farther. For this reason, many put down roots in the cities where they landed. They created huge ethnic ghettos, especially in New York City and Boston, Massachusetts. Ethnic ghettos are poor areas of a city where many people of the same race, religion, or ethnic background live.

For Irish immigrants, life in the United States was better than life in Ireland. But it was still harsh. The newcomers faced hostility and prejudice from native-born Americans. Many people viewed the Irish as "filthy, bad-tempered, and given to drink." By this time, large numbers of Protestants had shaped U.S. society. They rejected the efforts of Irish Catholics to establish separate Catholic schools for their children. Many Protestants saw these schools as evidence of unwillingness to Americanize. In addition, prejudice against the new immigrants limited their job opportunities.

Above: Irish emigrants wait on the dock in Queenstown, Ireland, to board ships bound for the United States. A potato famine in Ireland in the mid-1800s forced millions of people to leave their homeland in search of a better life.

Most Irish immigrants found jobs that required hard physical labor. For example, Irishwomen worked long hours in unsafe garment factories. Irishmen worked in mines. They also dug canals, paved roads, and built railroads. Irish laborers in the South "were sometimes considered more expendable [less valuable] than slaves and were hired at pitifully low wages for the dirtiest and most dangerous jobs, such as clearing snake-infested swamps." Irish immigrants usually held difficult, low-paying jobs that many native-born Americans wouldn't take. All the same, immigration foes often complained that immigrants took jobs from and lowered wages for native-born Americans.

THE KNOW NOTHINGS

In the mid-1800s, anti-immigration feeling in the United States led to a nativist movement. This movement worked against immigration. For example, the American Protective Association, an anti-Catholic society, protested Irish immigration. Some New York City nativists established the Nativist Party and published a newspaper called *Spirit of Seventy-Six*. The Nativist Party led to the American Republican Party, which in turn became the Native American Party. This party established branches in every New York and New Jersey county as well as in Boston and in Charleston, South Carolina.

As the nativist political movement spread, it became a national party. In 1855 it changed its name to the American Party. Members of the American Party were commonly called Know Nothings. (If asked about the secretive organization, members replied, "I know nothing.") The American Party supported severe limits on immigration—especially from Catholic countries. For example, the Know Nothings supported a wait of twenty-one years before immigrants could become U.S. citizens. Such a law would prevent immigrants from voting for a very long time. The American Party won widespread power in state and local elections in the 1850s.

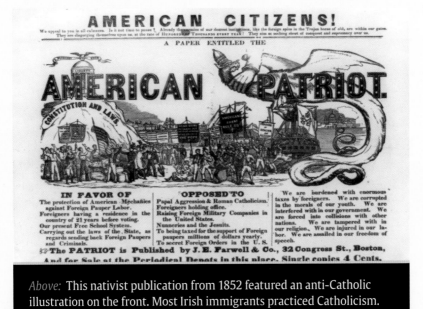

Above: This nativist publication from 1852 featured an anti-Catholic illustration on the front. Most Irish immigrants practiced Catholicism.

Why Americans love the Irish

From the Pages of
USA TODAY

ON MONDAY [St. Patrick's Day], tens of millions of Americans of every race and background will join together to celebrate a uniquely cherished ethnic holiday—a tribute to despised, destitute Hibernian [Irish] hordes whose descendants eventually claimed pride of place as the most popular of all immigrant groups. With mass immigration once again a contentious issue in our politics and culture, the St. Patrick's Day formula—combining Irish pride with unabashed, flag-waving Americanism—offers hope that current controversies might someday achieve similarly satisfactory resolution.

In part, we love the Irish because we instinctively embrace underdogs. The Emerald Isle suffered hellish torments during 800 years of oppression by the English—the same arrogant colonialists we defied in our own Revolution. When the starving Irish began to arrive en masse during "The Great Hunger" of the 1840s, they initially faced fiery hostility from nativist Americans and encountered occasional posted notices declaring, "No Irish Need Apply." Agitation culminated with [turmoil led to] bloody riots against churches and convents, with the virulently anti-immigrant "Know Nothing" Party electing numerous governors and mayors and even running a former president (Millard Fillmore) as a credible contender for the White House. Despite such obstacles, Irish arrivals persevered, establishing a vibrant Catholic community, dominating police and fire departments within a generation, and playing the lead role in organizing labor unions and big-city political machines.

When Harvard-educated millionaire John Fitzgerald Kennedy won the presidency in 1960, barely 110 years had passed since the American arrival of his famine-fleeing great-grandfather, Patrick Kennedy. That's the sort of poverty-to-power, rags-to-riches tale that has always inspired Americans in this nation of fresh starts and second chances.

The other key element in the appeal of the Irish involves their instantaneous affirmation [quick embrace] of American patriotism. Many other immigrant groups experienced a sense of divided loyalties. . . . In

Ireland, however, English overlords ruthlessly suppressed expressions of national pride or distinctive culture (including Gaelic language) so that immigrants embraced Yankee symbols and customs with scant hesitation.

German-Americans count as even more numerous than Irish-Americans (with 49 million claiming German ancestry, compared with 35 million saying they're Irish). But Ireland never became a rival world power or fought the United States in two brutal wars—preventing any contradiction between loyalty to origins and unquestioned love of the new homeland.

That same blend of heartfelt Americana and Emerald Isle nostalgia characterizes the annual revelry on St. Paddy's Day. Unlike other ethnic holidays, the festivities seem more familiar than exotic, more mainstream than multicultural. Irish names, accents and melodies have become inescapably American—not some demonstration of diversity or distinctive difference. Irishness feels comfortable, even cozy, in part because the sons of the Shamrock have been here so long (the first St. Patrick's Day Parade took place in New York in 1762) and most of them had arrived speaking English.

When St. Patrick's Day parades energize cities across the country, those processions feature marching bands, drill teams, floats and service clubs at least as likely to wave Cohan's Grand Old Flag [the U.S. flag] as to carry the green-white-and-orange of the republic of Ireland. In fact, the festive frenzy of this now international holiday mostly began in the USA, and then spread back across the ocean to Dublin and communities of Irish émigrés [emigrants] around the world.

More recent immigrant groups can surely benefit from the Irish-American example, understanding that the enthusiastic, unequivocal embrace of American identity need not undermine pride in heritage and kinship durable enough to flourish for centuries. Amid all the happy sailing on waves of foamy green beer, Irish-Americans (and fellow celebrants) acknowledge no inconsistency between remembering a distinctive history and cherishing American patriotism, and no clash of colors between shamrock green and the red, white and blue.

—Michael Medved, from the Opinion page

GERMAN IMMIGRANTS

At the same time Irish immigrants were arriving, German immigrants were also settling in the United States. About 1.5 million Germans had made their homes in the United States by 1860.

Unlike the Irish, who were fleeing poverty and starvation, the Germans were escaping political unrest. In the mid-1800s, Germany was not a single country. The German Confederation was an alliance of independent states. Efforts to unify the states into one German nation were failing. The political turmoil led to popular rebellion and several short wars. The conflict speeded German immigration to the United States.

Some German immigrants settled along the eastern seaboard. Large numbers also spread throughout the Midwest and Southwest to establish farming communities. Many towns—such as New Braunfels, Texas; Hermann, Missouri; and New Ulm, Minnesota—trace their heritage to these early German settlers. The founders of these towns named them after towns in Germany. So many German-speaking immigrants settled in Texas that it published a German edition of its laws in 1843.

Like the Irish, Germans experienced anti-immigrant hostility in the United States. Long after Benjamin Franklin had grumbled about German immigrants in Pennsylvania, native-born Americans were still grumbling. Nineteenth-century German immigrants tended to band together in German-speaking communities. The Germans seemed clannish to their English-speaking neighbors.

Religious factors also affected German immigrants. These Germans, like the Irish, were mainly Catholic. American nativists, especially the Know Nothings, argued that the U.S. government could not last if too many citizens owed loyalty to the pope. (The pope is the head of the worldwide Roman Catholic Church.)

Commenting on this and later eras, John Elson of *Time* magazine said, "The nativist sentiment that foreigners are somehow inferior to the American-born may be the nation's oldest and most persistent bias." Yet in spite of hardship,

The Opium Wars

The Opium Wars were two conflicts between the United Kingdom and China that took place during the mid-1800s. Prior to that time, China heavily restricted trade with other countries. The United Kingdom wanted to trade for Chinese goods, which were very valuable in Europe. But China believed the United Kingdom had little of value to offer in return.

To open up Chinese trade, the United Kingdom began shipping opium to China in the late 1700s. Opium is an addictive drug made from poppy seeds. China had banned opium imports except for medicinal use. But the United Kingdom had a lot of opium to sell from poppy farms in India, which was then a British colony. The United Kingdom smuggled opium into China, creating many Chinese opium addicts.

In 1839 China tightened its opium laws and destroyed about 2.4 million pounds (1.1 million kilograms) of British-owned opium stored in China. The United Kingdom launched the First Opium War in retaliation. The Second Opium War broke out in 1856, when China and the United Kingdom accused each other of breaking the treaty that had ended the First Opium War. The United Kingdom won both wars. In the peace treaties that ended the wars, the United Kingdom gained freer trade with China as well as large payments of silver and a new colony, Hong Kong.

criticism, and hostility, German immigrants persevered. And ultimately they too became woven into the fabric of U.S. society.

CHINESE AND JAPANESE IMMIGRANTS

Hundreds of thousands of immigrants from eastern Asian joined the newcomers from northern and western Europe. About three hundred thousand Chinese and ninety thousand Japanese came to the United States in the 1800s.

The first Chinese immigrants arrived in California during the early 1840s. Most were fleeing the turmoil of the Opium Wars (1839–1842 and

1856–1860) in China. Initially, the United States welcomed Chinese immigrants.

In the late 1840s, news of gold discoveries in California reached China. Chinese immigrants and sojourners began streaming across the Pacific Ocean. (Sojourners were temporary immigrants who intended to make money and return home.) By 1860 about twenty-four thousand Chinese were working in California's goldfields.

As the gold rush and the economy faltered, hostility toward Chinese immigrants began to grow. This hostility showed economically. For example, employers hired many Chinese miners to build the Central Pacific Railroad and to dig irrigation canals (for watering crops) in the Salinas and San Joaquin valleys of California. But wages for Chinese workers were only two-thirds of white workers' wages.

Hostility toward Chinese immigrants showed in U.S. laws too. In 1850 California passed a law to prevent racial intermarriage. Unlike European immigrants during the same

Above: Chinese workers helped build the Central Pacific Railroad across the western United States. This stretch of track, pictured in 1867, is in California's Sierra Nevadas.

period, the Chinese had no hope of gaining U.S. citizenship. The 1790 federal naturalization law had limited the privilege of citizenship to whites. Growing hostility from U.S. workers led to the Chinese Exclusion Act of 1882. This new law barred most Chinese workers (except teachers, diplomats, and merchants) from entering the United States. It also specifically forbade Chinese immigrants from becoming citizens. The law remained in effect for sixty-one years.

After the Chinese Exclusion Act passed, U.S. employers turned to Japan for cheap, temporary labor. In the mid-1800s, Japan was experiencing an economic depression. In addition, Japanese farmers were paying heavy taxes to fund the country's modernization. Many Japanese citizens who fell into poverty during this time hoped to earn money abroad as sojourners. Between 1885 and 1907, about 157,000 Japanese contract workers immigrated to California and to the sugarcane fields of Hawaii.

(Hawaii became a U.S. territory in 1898.)

Japanese immigrants, like the Chinese before them, faced nativist and racist hostility. For example, in 1906 the San Francisco, California, school board ordered separate classes for Japanese children. The Japanese government objected, and U.S. president Theodore Roosevelt called the move "a wicked absurdity." Roosevelt convinced the board to reverse its ruling.

In 1907 the government of Japan agreed to limit Japanese emigration rather than face a law like the Chinese Exclusion Act. That agreement ended immigration of Japanese laborers to the United States.

Two groups of Japanese remained in the United States, however. First-generation Japanese immigrants were called issei. Issei were legal residents and could stay in the United States legally. But they could not become citizens or own land because of their race. The children of issei were called nisei. Nisei were born in the United

States. Through the Fourteenth Amendment, they were automatically U.S. citizens. As citizens the nisei could own land and vote.

THE GOLDEN DOOR
SWINGS OPEN

In 1886 the people of France presented the Statue of Liberty to the United States. The gift was an expression of friendship and a symbol of the countries' shared ideal of liberty. The statue soon welcomed a new wave of immigrants. Between 1890 and 1920, twelve million immigrants arrived in the United States.

In 1890 the U.S. government started building a new immigration center on Ellis Island in New York Harbor. The government began using the Ellis Island immigration station in 1892. Immigrants waited in long lines there for questioning by government officials and examination by doctors. These new immigrants came from Italy, Russia, Ukraine, Lithuania, Latvia, Poland, Serbia, Bohemia, Slovakia, Croatia, Hungary, Greece, Syria, Spain, and Portugal.

Most of these immigrants left their homelands to escape poverty or persecution. For example, during the late 1800s and early 1900s, Russian Jews were targets of frequent pogroms. A pogrom was a type of riot—usually directed at Jewish

The Huddled Masses

Approximately one hundred million Americans—about 40 percent of the current U.S. population—trace their heritage to the wave of immigrants that arrived between 1890 and 1920. Most of these immigrants were greeted by the Statue of Liberty and entered the United States through Ellis Island in New York Harbor.

Above: An undated photo captures immigrants of European descent waiting to be processed at Ellis Island in New York.

communities—during which rioters destroyed synagogues (Jewish places of worship), homes, businesses, and schools and sometimes killed people. About 1.6 million Jews fled Russia, and 0.4 million Jews fled eastern Europe between 1892 and 1907.

Many new immigrants found living conditions in the United States only a little better than those they had left behind. These immigrants typically lived in cramped apartments in urban ghettos and worked at menial jobs. Immigrants did the backbreaking work of building railroads, paving streets, cutting stones, and mining coal. In his book *American Immigration*, author Gerald Leinwand notes:

> Those who came to America expecting quick riches were doomed to disappointment. In Sweden, farm workers earned $33.50 a year plus room and board. Little wonder that a salary of $40.00 a month in a coal mine, or $200.00 a year as a farmhand, was appealing. These figures by themselves do not tell the harsh desolation of the often storm-swept plains

of Kansas, Nebraska, Minnesota, and the Dakotas. They do not tell of the squalid conditions in factories where the immigrants worked and slums in which they lived, nor do they speak of the labor unions that resented the newcomers' presence and often refused them membership. But despite the hardships, most immigrants succeeded in America.

THE GOLDEN DOOR SLAMS SHUT

While these newcomers put down U.S. roots, anti-immigration forces worked to halt immigration. In the late 1800s, as in earlier periods, opposition to immigrants grew from economic concerns. It also stemmed from the idea that recent immigrants were somehow inferior to established residents.

In the 1890s, labor leaders began calling for a halt to unlimited immigration. Samuel Gompers, founder of the labor union known as the American Federation of Labor, was a Dutch Jew born in the United Kingdom. He migrated to the United States in 1863. Despite his own

Above: Samuel Gompers and his American Federation of Labor (AFL) were high-profile immigration foes. The AFL helped pass a number of anti-immigration laws in the late 1800s and early 1900s.

history, Gompers complained about new immigrants. "Both the intelligence and the prosperity of our working people are endangered by the present immigration," he said. "Cheap labor, ignorant labor, takes our jobs and cuts our wages."

concerned the group—and other nativists—was that immigrants from southern and eastern Europe might soon outnumber Americans of western European origin.

In 1907 President Roosevelt appointed a U.S. Immigration

> " **Both the intelligence and the prosperity of our working people are endangered by the present immigration. Cheap labor, ignorant labor, takes our jobs and cuts our wages.** "
>
> —**SAMUEL GOMPERS,** FOUNDER OF THE AMERICAN FEDERATION OF LABOR, 1902

In 1894 the Boston-based Immigration Restriction League formed. This group urged Congress to pass a law requiring that all immigrants be able to read and write, preferably in English. New Hampshire author and poet Thomas Bailey Aldrich supported this effort. He commented that the Immigration Restriction League wanted laws against "accents of menace alien to our air" (in other words, foreigners). What really

Commission to study the problem. Three years and one million dollars later, the commission issued a forty-one–volume report. According to the report, the new immigrants were indeed "inferior" to earlier arrivals. The report said that new immigrants did not assimilate (blend into U.S. culture) well. It also said the flood of immigrants decreased wages and job opportunities for native-born Americans.

The report and ongoing nativist political pressure led the U.S. government to restrict immigration. In 1921 Congress limited the number of immigrants from any single country to 3 percent of the foreign-born people of that nationality living in the United States in 1910. The limits did not apply to immigrants from Western Hemisphere (North and South American) countries.

The Johnson-Reed Act of 1924 reduced immigration even more drastically. The act set a quota (limit) for each Eastern Hemisphere (European, Asian, Australian, and African) nation at 2 percent of the 1890 foreign-born population of that nationality. Basing the quota on the 1890 census instead of the 1910 census gave preference to immigrants from northern and western Europe. In total, the quotas allowed only 165,000 new immigrants per year. These immigrants could also bring their wives and children, who wouldn't count toward the quotas.

The National Origins Act of 1929 set U.S. immigration policy until 1965. This act set a quota for each Eastern Hemisphere nationality based on its percentage of the general U.S. population in 1920. In total, the quotas allowed only 150,000 immigrants per year. Furthermore, the act required each immigrant to get a visa from a U.S. consul (government official) in the immigrant's country. (A visa is a government document letting an individual remain in the country ruled by that government for a certain length of time.) This requirement made it possible for immigration staff to screen and select potential immigrants.

During the next decade, immigration slowed. Strict immigration policies were firmly in place. The Great Depression (1929–1942) was paralyzing economies around the globe, making travel expensive and jobs scarce. Only about five hundred thousand immigrants arrived in the United States between 1930 and 1939. Six million had arrived in each of the two previous decades.

During World War II (1939–1945), U.S. immigration came nearly to a standstill. The War Brides Act of 1945 allowed entry to about 120,000 spouses and children of U.S. soldiers who had married while overseas. The Displaced Persons Acts of 1948 and 1950 let another 416,000 European refugees settle in the United States.

But U.S. politics became very conservative in the years right after World War II. Americans grew afraid of the Communist Soviet Union (a federation of fifteen republics including Russia), which was a political and military rival of the United States after the war. Americans also feared people in the United States who supported Communist thinking. The Internal Security Act of 1950 reflected this fear. The act increased the U.S. government's power to exclude and deport (expel) foreigners it considered dangerous to national security.

In 1952 Congress passed the McCarran-Walter Act (also called the Immigration and Nationality Act). It combined all the existing immigration laws into one law. This act further limited immigration, especially of Eastern Europeans with

Above: After the end of World War II, 555 Australian brides of U.S. servicemen immigrated, some with children, to the United States to join their husbands.

Communism

Communism is a political and economic theory developed in the mid-1800s by German philosophers Karl Marx and Friedrich Engels. Under Communism, a society abolishes private property and works to distribute a nation's riches equally among all its citizens. Under Communism individuals give up personal wealth and many personal freedoms, such as voting rights and the free and public practice of religion. In Communist nations, people do not own their own businesses or homes, elect their own leaders, or make their own political and economic decisions.

Many people around the world have found hope and promise in the Communist ideal of equality. In practice, however, Communism has often not lived up to that ideal. And in the years after World War II, the Communist Soviet Union and the democratic United States were fierce enemies. For this reason, most Americans disapproved strongly of Communism.

potential Communist ties. It set a quota of 160,000 immigrants per year from countries in Eastern Europe. Immigrants from northern and Western Europe filled more than 85 percent of the total immigration quota each year.

At the same time, the McCarran-Walter Act opened the door to some immigration from China and Japan. It also established special categories giving preference to immigrants with advanced education, technical skills, and other desirable qualities. Between 1956 and 1965, the United States gained seven thousand chemists, thirty-five thousand engineers, thirty-eight thousand nurses, and eighteen thousand doctors from various nations around the globe. In all, about 2.5 million immigrants arrived in the United States during the 1950s.

THE GOLDEN DOOR
CREAKS OPEN

In 1963 U.S. president John Kennedy sent an immigration reform bill to Congress. Kennedy wanted to repeal the nationality quota system. After Kennedy's assassination in November 1963, President Lyndon Johnson supported the same immigration policies.

The Hart-Celler Act (also called the Immigration and Nationality Act of 1965) ended quotas based on nationality. It established new quotas designed to achieve three main goals. These goals were to reunite families, open the United States to refugees, and attract skilled and talented people. The act set a limit of 290,000 immigrants annually—170,000 from the Eastern Hemisphere and 120,000 from the Western Hemisphere.

The Hart-Celler Act set seven "preference quotas." These quotas let certain kinds of immigrants enter the United States more easily than other kinds. First and second preference (40 percent) went to unmarried sons and daughters of U.S. citizens and legally admitted immigrants. Third preference (10 percent) was for members of the professions (such as medicine and engineering), scientists, and artists. Adult married children of U.S. citizens received fourth preference (10 percent). Fifth preference (24 percent) went to brothers and sisters of U.S. citizens. Sixth preference (10 percent) was for skilled labor or common laborers in short supply. Seventh preference (6 percent) was for refugees.

When President Johnson signed the 1965 legislation into law, he said it would "repair a very deep and painful flaw in the fabric of American justice.... The days of unlimited immigration are past. But those who do come will come because of what they are, and not because of the land from which they sprung."

Johnson and the authors of the 1965 act could not have foreseen the major shift in immigrant demographics. (Demographics are the traits of a population, such as nationality and economic status.) The end of the lengthy Vietnam War (1957–1975) caused thousands of refugees to flee Communist Vietnam and Cambodia. By late 1975, the United States had admitted 130,000 Vietnamese and

Cambodians under special quota exemptions. About twenty years later, nearly 600,000 Southeast Asian refugees were living in the United States. During the same period, immigration from Asia, the Middle East, Africa, and Latin America steadily increased. Meanwhile, European immigration steadily declined.

The first major change to the 1965 Hart-Celler Act occurred in 1980. In that year, U.S. president Jimmy Carter signed the Refugee Act into law. The law defined a refugee as anyone who could not remain in his or her home country because of a well-founded fear of persecution on the basis of race,

LEGAL IMMIGRATION IN THE 1980s
Total legal immigrants in the United States: 7.3 million

By Region
From Latin America: 3.7 million
From Asia: 2.7 million
From the Caribbean: 872,000
From Europe: 761,500
From Central America: 468,000
From Africa: 177,000

By Country
From Mexico: 1.7 million
From the Philippines: 549,000
From Taiwan: 346,000
From South Korea: 334,000
From Vietnam: 281,000
From India: 250,000
From Iran: 116,000
From Laos: 112,000
From China: 98,000

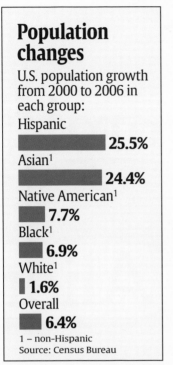

Population changes

U.S. population growth from 2000 to 2006 in each group:

Hispanic
25.5%

Asian[1]
24.4%

Native American[1]
7.7%

Black[1]
6.9%

White[1]
1.6%

Overall
6.4%

1 – non-Hispanic
Source: Census Bureau

By Julie Snider, USA TODAY, 2007

religion, nationality, or political opinion. The 1980 law ended the Hart-Celler Act's refugee quota of 17,400 per year (the seventh preference quota). The new law allowed up to 50,000 refugees per year into the United States.

More could enter if they could demonstrate "grave, humanitarian reasons." At the same time, the quota for other immigrants dropped from 290,000 to 270,000 per year.

According to a December 1989 *USA TODAY* article, the U.S. population grew nearly 10 percent from 1980 to 1989. That's a gain of 22 million people. One-quarter of that gain happened in California, due mostly to domestic and international immigration. Population Reference Bureau demographer William O'Hare predicted, "This will have subtle changes on what political issues get on the national agenda in Congress." Reporter William Dunn in turn alerted readers, "Watch for Sun Belt [southern and southwestern United States] issues such as water supply and immigration to go onto the front burner."

CHAPTER TWO

Modern U.S. Immigration Policy

MODERN U.S. IMMIGRATION POLICY RESTS PRIMARily on two laws passed in 1996. They are the Illegal Immigration Reform and Immigrant Responsibility Act (IIRIRA) and the Personal Responsibility and Work Opportunity Reconciliation Act (PRWORA). Both measures passed only after a long—and often explosive—debate that began in 1995.

IMMIGRATION REFORM IN THE 1990s

In the 1990s, anti-immigration sentiment in the United States was at fever pitch. Many people around the country were working to restrict immigration and to limit benefits and services to immigrants. In addition, many politicians were eager to cut social service budgets. They hoped such budget cuts would pave the way for tax cuts, an idea that was very popular at the time. The anti-immigration and budget-cutting trends came together in two major bills related to immigration: IIRIRA and PRWORA. IIRIRA was an immigration

Left: During a protest against illegal immigrants in Houston, Texas, in 2006, a woman holds up a sign supporting legal immigrants but opposing those who enter the country illegally.

reform bill. PRWORA was a welfare reform bill.

While Congress wrangled over these bills, some members suggested harsh provisions. For example, one IIRIRA proposal would have banned the children of illegal immigrants from attending public schools. Elton Gallegly, a Republican congressman from California, authored this proposal. He saw it as a way to fight illegal immigration.

Opponents of Gallegly's measure argued that it would punish the wrong people. Instead of targeting parents who had decided to enter this country illegally, it targeted their children, who had no choice in the matter. Lawmakers withdrew the amendment before President Bill Clinton signed the bill into law.

Another proposal would have given federal immigration officials the power to deport legal immigrants who used more than one year's worth of government services during their first seven years of residency. These services included subsidized (government-funded) housing and child care. Supporters of the proposal, such as Republican congressman Lamar Smith of

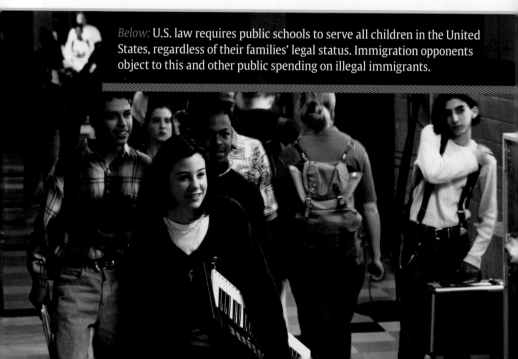

Below: U.S. law requires public schools to serve all children in the United States, regardless of their families' legal status. Immigration opponents object to this and other public spending on illegal immigrants.

Texas, said that both legal and illegal immigrants abuse government benefits. "We will continue to keep the welcome mat out. We just are not going to be a doormat anymore," Smith explained.

food stamps (to buy food) and Supplemental Security Income (SSI), a cash benefit for the elderly and the disabled. The bill cut spending on food stamps by 14 percent, or twenty-seven billion dollars, over six years. Legal

> ❝ **This bill does more to hurt American citizens and legal immigrants than it does to stop illegal immigration.** ❞
>
> **—SENATOR TED KENNEDY,**
> REFERRING TO IIRIRA, 1996

Senator Ted Kennedy disagreed. He said, "This bill does more to hurt American citizens and legal immigrants than it does to stop illegal immigration." Paul Simon, a Democratic senator from Illinois, called the measure "deeply flawed." Congress removed the deportation proposal before passing the bill.

PRWORA, though not strictly an immigration bill, nonetheless aimed to restrict many federal benefits available to immigrants. These benefits include

immigrants could no longer receive food stamps or SSI during their first ten years in the United States. The bill denied benefits to all illegal immigrants.

Republican sponsors of PRWORA argued that the cost of food stamps had gotten out of control. When the act passed, twenty-seven million Americans—one out of every ten—received food stamps. Congressman Pat Roberts, a Kansas Republican, said, "We wanted to take the program off the automatic spending pilot."

Opponents of PRWORA feared the new law would only increase hunger in poor communities. Robert Greenstein, executive director of the Center on Budget and Policy Priorities, said, "Cuts of this magnitude [size] are unprecedented. Not even during the early years of the [President Ronald] Reagan administration [1981–1989, a period in which government cut budgets for many social services] have there ever been cuts approaching these in depth and breadth. They will affect every poor family and every individual on food stamps."

PRWORA passed into law in August 1996. Among its many provisions, the following strongly affected immigrants:

- Legal immigrants who are not U.S. military veterans or have not worked and paid taxes in the United States for at least ten years may not receive SSI or food stamps.
- Legal immigrants who arrived after August 22, 1996, may not receive most federal benefits during their first five years in the country.
- After five years, new immigrants who have sponsors must include their sponsors' income when applying for federal benefits. (Sponsors are immediate relatives who are U.S. citizens. A sponsor agrees to support an immigrant for a specific period of time.)
- Illegal immigrant children *are* eligible for school lunch programs.
- Illegal immigrants may not receive federal, state, or local public benefits.

IIRIRA passed into law in September 1996. Its main provisions are as follows:

- No more than 675,000 legal immigrants may enter the United States annually.
- Approximately one hundred thousand refugees may enter the United States each year. This figure can fluctuate. Lawmakers review it annually.

- Relatives of legal immigrants eligible to immigrate are parents, children, siblings, and spouses of siblings.
- A legal immigrant or citizen wishing to sponsor a foreign relative must have an annual household income of $19,500. (This is the 1996 poverty level of $15,600 for a family of four, plus $3,900.) The income requirement ensures that the sponsoring family would be able to support a legal immigrant until the new arrival becomes self-sufficient.

TWENTY-FIRST CENTURY EFFORTS

On September 11, 2001, nineteen terrorists hijacked four U.S. airliners. They intentionally crashed these planes into the twin towers of New York City's World Trade Center and into the Pentagon (U.S.

Above: Smoke billows out of the World Trade Center towers in New York after terrorists hijacked two airplanes and flew them into the buildings on September 11, 2001. The attack by foreigners on U.S. soil that day forever changed the way the U.S. government oversees immigration policy.

Department of Defense headquarters near Washington, D.C.). The fourth plane crashed in rural Pennsylvania after its passengers tried to wrest control from the hijackers. The attacks killed about three thousand people, including all the hijackers, all the passengers, and many hundreds of people on the ground and inside the buildings.

In response to these attacks, the U.S. government passed the USA PATRIOT Act on October 26, 2001. The acronym *USA PATRIOT* stands for "Uniting and Strengthening America by Providing Appropriate Tools Required to Intercept and Obstruct Terrorism." Americans commonly call this law simply the Patriot Act. Its purpose is to prevent future terrorist attacks in the United States and abroad. If the U.S. government suspects its residents—citizens or noncitizens—are involved in terrorist activities, it can expand its authority to investigate the suspicion.

The Patriot Act, though not an immigration law, has dramatically affected immigrants in the United States. In an effort to provide security, the law permits the government to take some actions that Americans once considered unacceptable or controversial. For example, the Patriot Act has increased the power of federal officials to track down illegal immigrants with terrorist ties. Using Federal Bureau of Investigation (FBI) data, U.S. Citizenship and Immigration Services can check the criminal history of visa applicants. USCIS can deny entry to the spouses and children of illegal immigrants who have terrorist ties. The United States can hold illegal immigrants accused of terrorist ties indefinitely with no access to legal help. The Patriot Act requires detailed tracking of U.S. entries and exits. The government must approve foreign students who wish to attend flight schools, vocational schools, and language training schools in the United States. Overall, the Patriot Act has made it more difficult for noncitizens to gain visas, work permits, legal residency, and citizenship.

COMPREHENSIVE
IMMIGRATION
REFORM

THE ONLY WAY TO FIX
OUR BROKEN SYSTEM

Above: Senators John McCain (R-AZ) *(left)* and Edward Kennedy (D-MA) *(right)* speak at a press conference about immigration in June 2006.

With new concerns about national security and ongoing concerns about the cultural and economic effects of immigration, Congress once again tackled immigration reform. A March 2006 *USA TODAY* editorial observed, "Pressures to revisit the issue run in cycles, usually paralleling anxiety about the economy, jobs and national security. When concern slackens, businesses become reliant on cheap labor, consumers welcome the lower prices for food and services, and enforcement is gradually neglected."

A bipartisan (a joint two-party) effort to hammer out new immigration laws began in 2006. Senator John McCain, an Arizona Republican, and Senator Ted Kennedy cosponsored a bill with strong support from President George W. Bush. This bill would have granted amnesty to illegal immigrants—a chance to remain in the United States legally and seek citizenship. At the time, a *USA TODAY*–Gallup poll showed 78 percent of respondents felt that illegal immigrants should receive a chance at citizenship.

No more hollow solutions

From the Pages of
USA TODAY

FOR SOME OF THE most hard-core, anti-immigrant Republican candidates, who thought they had a surefire political winner, a funny thing happened on the way to the elections.

They lost.

In states from Indiana to Arizona, immigrant bashing didn't play well. In a nationwide exit poll Nov. 7, 57% of voters said most illegal immigrants in the USA should be offered a path to legal status, and just 38% favored deportation.

The hard-liners' defeat clears the way for a more balanced reform of the immigration system that wasn't possible just nine days ago and that the nation desperately needs.

At his post-election news conference, President Bush allowed that he might well "find some common ground" with Democrats on this issue. In another sign of the shifting political climate, a moderate on immigration, Cuban-born Sen. Mel Martinez of Florida, was named as the new chairman of the Republican National Committee.

Since last year, it has been clear that Bush and many Democrats agree on the outlines of a program to enforce the law, create some kind of guest-worker program and provide a path to legalization for millions of illegal immigrants already in the USA.

Yet history shows that it's one thing to pass an immigration law and quite another to do anything meaningful about the problem.

In the past two decades, Congress has approved supposedly sweeping new immigration measures every 10 years. Both turned out to be charades.

The number of illegal aliens in the USA—about 12 million today, nearly five times as many as in 1989—attests to the emptiness of those efforts. Each time, the government failed to establish a guest-worker program or to provide the money and means to enforce the law.

The bulk of funds was poured into border enforcement instead of deterrents to illegal employment, the magnet that draws migrants to the USA. When, in 1998, the Clinton administration cracked down effectively on employers who were hiring illegal workers, the businesses and their allies in Congress, as well as immigration advocates and unions, squawked so much that the program was scrapped.

For this time to be any different, lawmakers will have to withstand pressure to create a system so weak that it pleases the majority and accomplishes nothing. Political victories are fleeting. Another failure would only ignite a new backlash with a draconian [cruel] result.

Further, if there is to be a path to legalization for millions of undocumented people already here, the system must work far better than Citizenship and Immigration Services does now. Just look at our letters to the editor today, and you'll get a sense of the frustrating, expensive, bureaucratic morass [maze] that confronts people who seek to obey U.S. immigration laws.

Last week's elections provide Bush and the Democratic-controlled Congress with an opportunity to pass a historic immigration reform. But they'll have to buck a long history of pretend solutions to do it right.

— USA TODAY editors

Kennedy commented, "As with so many issues, the American people are ahead of Washington on immigration reform. They know that only a plan that offers a path to earned citizenship will fix our broken system."

In this statement, Kennedy referred to a goal many employers and politicians shared. They wanted to meet the needs of service, factory, and farming industries by legalizing all the illegal immigrant labor that fuels them. In addition, these people believed that amnesty was the only practical solution for dealing with the United States' huge population of illegal immigrants. Deporting them would not only harm the economy, it would also be very expensive.

But conservative politicians strongly opposed any path to

Above: Guadalupe Adams *(right)* is a coordinator at CASA de Maryland in Silver Spring, Maryland. Her organization helps men and women find jobs. Most of the people she helps are immigrants from Latin America.

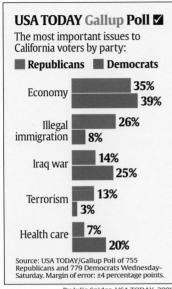

USA TODAY Gallup Poll ☑

The most important issues to
California voters by party:

■ Republicans   ■ Democrats

Economy   35%
           39%

Illegal   26%
immigration   8%

Iraq war   14%
            25%

Terrorism   13%
             3%

Health care   7%
               20%

Source: USA TODAY/Gallup Poll of 755
Republicans and 779 Democrats Wednesday-
Saturday. Margin of error: ±4 percentage points.

By Julie Snider, USA TODAY, 2008

citizenship for illegal immigrants. Brian Bilbray, a Republican representative from California, summed up a common attitude among conservative thinkers: "You'd be rewarding them for breaking our laws."

The bipartisan effort began to unravel in April 2007 when McCain "stepped back from the leadership role he had played in the talks" to focus on his 2008 presidential campaign. At the time, Republicans who opposed the bill were pressuring McCain heavily to withdraw his support for amnesty. Gary Kirk, a Republican fund-raiser, noted, "Even in his own state of Arizona, 60 percent of the people oppose the amnesty for illegal aliens [immigrants] that he favors. Frank Sharry of the National Immigration Forum, a pro-immigration group, told reporters that McCain's absence "destabilizes the debate." The immigration bill died in the Senate on June 28, 2007.

In August 2007, a *USA TODAY* editorial commented on the issue. It observed that the bill's demise had caused states and communities across the country to take matters into their own hands. It cited dozens of new state and local laws. Many of the measures seemed reasonable, said the editors. Illegal immigrants do stream across U.S. borders. Many enter legally but overstay their visas. Businesses ignore laws against hiring illegals. Many of the United States' twelve million illegal immigrants place a burden on local schools and hospitals. But "trying to fix this huge mess piecemeal makes no more sense than each state and city adopting its own foreign policy.

Immigration overhaul crumbles in Senate vote

From the Pages of
USA TODAY

WASHINGTON—An outpouring of opposition and a campaign cycle on fast-forward overcame a powerful alliance of key Democratic and Republican leaders, as a sweeping immigration bill collapsed Thursday in the Senate.

A move to limit the immigration debate and bring the bill to a final vote failed 46–53. The vote halts one of President Bush's top domestic priorities and leaves unresolved the fate of an estimated 12 million illegal immigrants now living in what Sen. Ken Salazar, D-Colo., called "a system of victimization."

It also raises questions about the prospects for legislative accomplishment in a Congress faced with a contentious [conflict-laden] agenda on Iraq, climate change, taxes and budget issues.

"A lot of us worked hard to see if we couldn't find common ground," Bush said. "It didn't work."

Senate Majority Leader Harry Reid, D-Nev., called the vote "really disheartening."

The bill's defeat came despite an enormous investment of time and political capital by senior Democrats and Republicans.

Opponents claimed a populist victory over what Roy Beck of NumbersUSA called "the cheap-labor lobby." Beck said his organization, which focuses on immigration-related issues, generated more than 2 million faxes against the immigration bill since May. Hours before the Senate vote, the Capitol switchboard was swamped with phone calls.

"The intensity level and the passions on this bill, we've never seen anything like it. Not even close," said Sen. John Ensign, R-Nev., who voted against the bill despite a call from Bush.

Ensign also chairs the National Republican Senatorial Committee. Eleven senators—four Democrats and seven Republicans—who voted in favor of last year's Senate immigration bill, which died in the House

[U.S. House of Representatives], voted against this year's version. All of them are up for re-election in 2008.

Among them was Senate Minority Leader Mitch McConnell, R-Ky. In a Senate speech earlier this month, McConnell said, "I am in favor of trying to pass an immigration bill." On Thursday, after voting against it, he said he was responding to an outcry from Republicans, including those in his home state.

Sen. Lindsey Graham, R-S.C., said politics played a role in the bill's defeat: "Some of it was pressure."

Opposition was bipartisan, running the gamut from the AFL-CIO [a federation of labor unions] to the Minuteman Civil Defense Corps, a citizen border patrol group.

The bill would have beefed up border security, expanded opportunities for foreigners to take temporary jobs in the USA and made job qualifications a factor in selecting immigrants. It also would have put about 12 million illegal immigrants on a path to citizenship.

Graham predicted that Congress's failure to address immigration will lead to a patchwork of state and municipal ordinances [city laws] as local governments attempt to fill the void. According to the National Conference of State Legislatures, at least 1,169 immigration measures were introduced in 50 state legislatures as of April.

Commerce Secretary Carlos Gutierrez said attitudes appear to have changed since he "felt so welcome" arriving in the USA as a Cuban refugee. "I hope that the day will return," he said, "when we will once again think about immigration not as something to tolerate but as something to be proud of."

—Kathy Kiely

> " **I hope that the day will return when we will once again think about immigration not as something to tolerate but as something to be proud of.** "
>
> —**CARLOS GUTIERREZ,** U.S. COMMERCE SECRETARY AND CUBAN IMMIGRANT
> **USA TODAY · AUGUST 15, 2007**

Immigration is a huge national problem that requires a comprehensive national solution. Local laws will just move people from one community or state to the next where the environment is less hostile, or they'll burrow even deeper into the underground economy. Few are likely to leave the country."

WHO OVERSEES U.S. IMMIGRATION?

The U.S. government formed the Department of Homeland Security in November 2002 in response to the September 2001 terrorist attacks. Unlike the Department of Defense, which handles military actions, DHS works in the civilian sphere to protect the United States. Its goal is to prepare for, prevent, and respond to domestic emergencies—especially terrorism. The new department brought together twenty-two federal agencies to more efficiently oversee U.S. security. These agencies include those that manage immigration and other traffic into the United States. Among other things, DHS is in charge of providing immigration services and enforcing immigration law in the United States. DHS performs these tasks through three agencies:

- U.S. Citizenship and Immigration Services processes and decides citizenship, permanent resident, refugee, visa, and asylum applications. (Asylum is protection from arrest and removal given by one country to a refugee from another country.)

- U.S. Customs and Border Protection (CBP) protects U.S. entry points from terrorism, human and drug smuggling, illegal immigration, and agricultural pests while assisting legal travel and trade.
- U.S. Immigration and Customs Enforcement (ICE) identifies, investigates, and dismantles security weaknesses in the U.S. border, infrastructure (public works such as roads and bridges), and transportation and financial systems.

LEGAL IMMIGRATION

All immigrants must possess a Lawful Permanent Resident card. This is an identification card issued by USCIS. The card is commonly called a green card. It allows an immigrant to live and work in the United States legally. Green cards are valid for ten years and are renewable.

Before anyone can legally immigrate to the United States, a prospective employer in the United States or a relative who is a U.S.

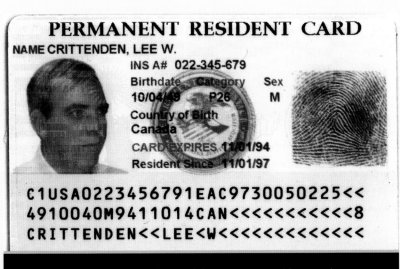

Above: This is an example of a Lawful Permanent Resident card, or a green card. An immigrant must have this card to live and work in the United States legally.

citizen must file an immigrant petition with USCIS on behalf of the immigrant. If USCIS approves the petition, the immigrant must then wait for an immigrant visa number to become available.

After an immigrant visa number becomes available and before entering the United States, the applicant may apply to USCIS to change his or her current status to resident status. Or the applicant may apply to the Department of State for an immigrant visa. Immediate family members (spouses, minor children, and parents) of U.S. citizens receive preference in the process. So do priority workers, such as people with extraordinary ability in science, art, education, business, or athletics. Others, such as skilled workers and married children of U.S.

citizens, face a long wait ranging from five to eleven years.

NATURALIZATION

To apply for U.S. citizenship, an immigrant must be at least eighteen years old and must have been a legal resident of the United States for at least five years. The applicant must also be able to read, write, and speak English, unless he or she is over fifty years old and has been a legal resident for twenty years or more.

The naturalization process begins with an application to USCIS. The application includes collecting

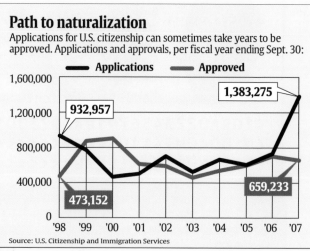

Path to naturalization

Applications for U.S. citizenship can sometimes take years to be approved. Applications and approvals, per fiscal year ending Sept. 30:

━━ Applications   ━━ Approved

1,600,000

1,383,275

1,200,000   932,957

800,000

400,000   473,152   659,233

0   '98 '99 '00 '01 '02 '03 '04 '05 '06 '07

Source: U.S. Citizenship and Immigration Services

By Julie Snider, USA TODAY, 2008

Above: U.S. residents Cao Mao Sun *(right)* and Huang Zhen Qiu *(left),* originally from China, take a citizenship class in Houston, Texas.

fingerprints, a blood or tissue sample, and background information, including criminal history. With two U.S. citizens present as witnesses, the applicant offers proof of age, residence, character, and education. He or she then takes written and oral tests to show a basic understanding of U.S. history and government.

The U.S. citizenship test is a standardized exam with multiple-choice and short-answer written sections as well as an oral interview. Candidates receive preparation packets that include sample questions. They also receive a list of vocabulary study words.

Later, at a final hearing, a judge reviews the application and test results. He or she listens to the recommendations of a USCIS officer and decides whether to grant citizenship

Above: On March 1, 2009, more than one thousand people from more than fifty countries took the U.S. citizenship oath in El Paso, Texas.

to the candidate. If the judge approves the candidate, he or she attends a naturalization ceremony. At this ceremony, the candidate takes an oath of allegiance to the United States and receives a certificate of naturalization.

Naturalized citizens enjoy the same rights that native-born citizens do, with one exception. A naturalized citizen cannot be president or vice president of the United States.

ILLEGAL IMMIGRATION

A citizen of another country living in the United States without a green card is an illegal immigrant. The number of illegal immigrants in the United States is unknown. Recent estimates place the number at about twelve million people. This is about one-third of the roughly thirty-five million immigrants living in the United States in the early twenty-first century.

Illegal immigrants can slip into the United States by various means. A large portion of illegal immigrants comes from and through Mexico. Many simply run or swim across unguarded parts of the vast United States–Mexico border. Other illegals enter U.S. airports with forged documents. Still others remain in the United States after their tourist visas expire.

U.S. officials can automatically deport any illegal immigrant they find. But illegal immigrants often evade discovery. They blend easily into ethnic communities, find work, and stay on as undocumented (informal) workers. The number of illegal immigrants is very high compared to the number of ICE officials. So the government has great difficulty effectively managing the situation.

Above: In San Ysidro, California, officials stop a car trying to smuggle five illegal immigrants across the U.S.–Mexico border.

Nearly all illegal immigrants come to the United States to work and save money. Most come from very poor countries, where job opportunities are few. Although some find good jobs in the United States, most work for low pay, long hours, and no benefits. Even in low-paying jobs, illegal workers can usually earn more than they could in their own countries.

Illegal immigrants have few rights or protections under U.S. law. But hospitals that participate in Medicaid (a government-funded health-care program for the poor)—in other words, almost all hospitals—must give illegal immigrants emergency medical care. By law, these hospitals may not refuse emergency treatment to anyone, regardless of citizenship status or ability to pay. Children who are illegal immigrants are allowed to attend public schools. And according to the Fourteenth Amendment to the Constitution, any child born on U.S. soil—regardless of the parents' legal status—is automatically a U.S. citizen.

Over the years, many efforts to repeal the Fourteenth Amendment have occurred. For example, Bill McCollum, a Florida representative, successfully introduced a Fourteenth

Above: Hospitals and clinics can refuse non-emergency medical care to illegal immigrants such as Juana *(above)* and her three young sons.

Amendment revision to the Republican Party platform (statement of beliefs) in 1996. An aide to McCollum, Karl Kaufmann, explained that when the Fourteenth Amendment was written, neither immigration laws nor illegal immigrants existed. The Fourteenth Amendment's purpose was to grant citizenship to and prevent discrimination against former slaves. He went on to say that modern opponents of the Fourteenth Amendment hoped to end birthright citizenship to the children of illegal immigrants. "People come here illegally," Kaufmann said. "They run across the border, give birth, and suddenly, that child is a citizen, and eligible for all sorts of benefits. Children of illegal aliens should be considered aliens as well. They should not be considered citizens merely because their parents were successful at evading U.S. law."

Repeal of the Fourteenth Amendment has never gained national support. All the same, it is a popular subject of blogs in the twenty-first century and remains one of many anti-immigration banners that fly across the country. With outdated immigration laws in place and a heated social and political debate regarding immigration raging, it's unlikely that the issue will fade in the near future.

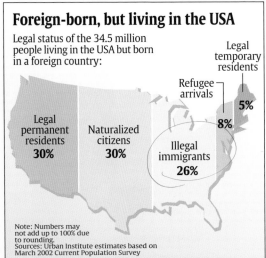

USA TODAY Snapshots®

Foreign-born, but living in the USA

Legal status of the 34.5 million people living in the USA but born in a foreign country:

Legal permanent residents **30%**

Naturalized citizens **30%**

Illegal immigrants **26%**

Refugee arrivals

Legal temporary residents **5%**

8%

Note: Numbers may not add up to 100% due to rounding.
Sources: Urban Institute estimates based on March 2002 Current Population Survey

By Shannon Reilly and Alejandro Gonzalez, USA TODAY, 2004

CHAPTER THREE

A Country Divided

IN THE ABSENCE OF A UNIFIED FEDERAL IMMIGRATION policy, states, counties, and cities around the country have enacted their own laws to manage immigration issues. Different communities deal with immigration differently. This creates vastly different conditions throughout the nation. Immigrants in some states, where laws are harsh and regularly enforced, may live in constant fear of arrest and deportation. In other states, immigration law may be looser and enforced only randomly. Laws often reflect the economic realities in communities. In some cases, communities may have very few jobs or limited budgets for social services. These communities may be less tolerant of immigration. In other situations, a city may have a great need for immigrant labor, and laws there may be more forgiving. Whatever the case, policies vary widely and the legal system has trouble keeping up.

Left: This neighborhood in New York City has a high Asian population and attracts Asian immigrants. Different U.S. cities, counties, and states have different immigration laws.

A PATCHWORK OF LOCAL LAWS

One such instance of shifting local laws occurred after the September 2001 terrorist attacks. Many illegal immigrants living in New York City fled to eastern Pennsylvania's Pocono Mountains. They knew that local and federal authorities would be focusing hard on finding and deporting illegals, because some of the September 11 terrorists had been in the United States illegally. Many immigrants fleeing New York came to Hazleton, a northeastern Pennsylvania city of twenty-three thousand people.

As a result of this influx of new people, Hazleton mayor Lou Barletta made headlines five years later. He proposed a city law to drive out illegal immigrants. Barletta championed the law because he said illegal immigrants had caused a crime wave in Hazleton and had strained public services. "What I'm doing here is protecting the legal taxpayer of any race," said Barletta. "And I will get rid of the illegal people. It's this simple: *They must leave.*"

Hazleton's city council approved the law (the Illegal Immigrant Relief Act) in July 2006. The new law placed fines on landlords who rented to illegal immigrants. It yanked business licenses from employers who hired undocumented workers. The law also made English Hazleton's official language. It forbade employees to translate documents into another language without official authorization.

> " **What I'm doing here is protecting the legal taxpayer of any race. And I will get rid of the illegal people. It's this simple:** *They must leave.* "
>
> —LOU BARLETTA,
> MAYOR OF HAZLETON, PENNSYLVANIA, 2006

Hazleton's new law heated the city's simmering tensions to a boil. For example, a police car often parked across the street from a Mexican restaurant in town. The presence of the police intimidated customers, who slowly stopped coming to the restaurant. The owner, a longtime legal resident, lost so much business that he had to close the restaurant. When Amilcar Arroyo, the publisher of a local Spanish-language newspaper, attended a rally supporting the new law, the crowd turned on him. They yelled, "Get out of the country!" Arroyo, a U.S. citizen from Peru, is a longtime resident of Hazleton. Police escorted him to safety.

Above: Peruvian native Amilcar Arroyo is the editor of *El Mensajero*, a Spanish-language newspaper in Hazelton, Pennsylvania. In 2006 Arroyo supported a new law against immigration passed by Mayor Barletta. The law's opponents see underlying racism in anti-immigration legislation such as this.

"Those people didn't see me as a person," said Arroyo. Opponents of Hazleton's law agree. They say it's racist, hateful, and unnecessary. Local resident Alan Frank believed Barletta was using the law as a tool to advance his political career. "He's a small-town mayor who thinks he can build his political base by playing on people's fears of immigrants, said Frank. "He's going to lose the court case and use millions of dollars to fight it—money he could have used for the social services that he says these people are sucking up."

A federal court struck down Hazleton's law in July 2007. The judge ruled that it interfered with federal immigration law. The judge also said that the law violated the due process rights of employers, landlords, and illegal immigrants. Due process means that laws may not contain provisions that result in the unfair, arbitrary, or unreasonable treatment of an individual. Barletta appealed the decision.

Barletta's law lost the court battle, but it won nationwide publicity. Barletta won reelection as mayor in November 2007 by 90 percent of the vote. "I've been a voice for many people," he said. Barletta also ran for the U.S. House of Representatives in 2008. He lost that race by 4 percent of the vote.

Immigration tensions have reached deep into the U.S. heartland. Austin, Minnesota, lies 1,050 miles (1,690 km) west of Hazleton. The cities have much in common. Both have populations of about twenty-three thousand. Both have large immigrant communities.

Austin's Hispanic (Latin American) population has grown over the years. The 1990 census showed fewer than two hundred Hispanic residents in Austin. Twenty years later, that number has grown to five thousand. According to Mayor Tom Stiehm, at least three-fourths of Austin's Hispanic residents are there illegally. Many work for the city's two largest employers, Hormel Foods and Quality Pork Processors.

In the mid-1900s, meat-packing workers in the United States were well organized and well paid for the hazardous and unpleasant labor they did. "Apparently conditions were too good from the perspective of the companies," noted Joel Dyer, publisher of the *Fort Collins Weekly*, a Colorado newspaper. From the 1960s to the 1980s, the industry restructured to gain the upper hand. Companies merged to increase their size and their financial clout. They moved their plants from urban to rural areas, where labor was cheaper. They forced unions to organize plant by plant, which weakened

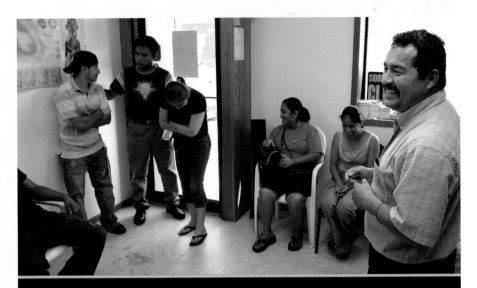

Above: Victor Contreras *(right),* organizer for Centro Campesino, jokes with other immigrants. The organization in Austin, Minnesota, helps migrant workers adjust to their new life in the United States.

their bargaining power. When union workers launched strikes, the companies brought in low-paid, nonunion immigrant workers to pick up the slack. The immigrants stayed. Eventually the unions gave up on the meatpacking industry.

In the twenty-first century, the meatpacking industry relies largely on low-paid, nonunion workers. Many of these workers are illegal immigrants. By paying lower wages and hiring illegal immigrants, meatpackers

can increase their profits. They can push their production lines faster and let safety standards slip. Undocumented workers seldom complain, for fear of deportation. Though meatpacking jobs typically pay low wages, the pay is often far better than an illegal immigrant's potential earnings at home.

The willingness of the meatpacking industry to hire undocumented workers draws illegal immigrants in huge numbers. The same is true of various other

Above: Somali refugee Farton Osman trims beef at a meatpacking plant in Emporia, Kansas. To increase profits, the meatpacking industry hires many low-wage immigrants. This approach has raised concerns with labor unions and immigration opponents.

hazardous, tedious, difficult, unpleasant, and/or seasonal jobs. Many illegal immigrants work as hotel maids, short-order cooks, waiters, gardeners, seamstresses, fruit and vegetable pickers, and construction hands. None of these jobs pays well. But for desperately poor immigrants, all of these jobs provide a path to a better life.

In August 2008, a group called Minnesotans Seeking Immigration Reform held a forum in Austin. The gathering drew 150 people, virtually all of them Anglos (non-Hispanic white people). Ruthie Hendrycks, the group's leader, said that if the United States doesn't enforce its immigration laws, "anarchy [lawlessness] is going to come." She added, "How many of us can commit a crime and get away with it?" Linnea Burtch, who helped organize the meeting, believes the United States can force illegal immigrants to leave. "All we want is to do what's right," she said. "It's not a race issue. It's a legal issue."

At Jerry's Card Room, an Austin baseball card shop, customers agree: Hispanic immigrants are welcome, but only if they're legal. "If they're not, ship them out," said John Leachman, a retired Hormel Foods meatpacking plant employee. Jerry Salisbury, the shop's owner, says, "I agree with deporting the illegals. I agree with that 100 percent."

Austin resident Jim Stiles, owner of Super Fresh Produce, takes a moderate view of the issue. Stiles says, "It's obvious that we need these workers and the majority of them are hardworking people with families." However, he adds, "There's a lot of resentment. Some people complain when Hispanics move next door and object to the social services they receive. We need to keep talking about it. It's just [a question of] knocking down those [cultural] barriers."

People like Vicki Trimble, who owns a flower shop in Austin, don't believe that hostility and harsh measures are the answer. Acceptance "will come

Above: In August 2008, residents of Austin, Minnesota, gathered at an anti-immigration meeting. The city's Hispanic population grew 69 percent between 2000 and 2006 as immigrants came for jobs at the city's meatpacking plants.

Challenging Common Perceptions

New York attorney Raul Reyes is a *USA TODAY* columnist. In December 2007, he wrote that there is "a common attitude among those who actively demonize immigrants [portray them as evil]." He explained, "Opposing illegal immigrants requires little beyond repeating familiar complaints: Undocumented workers are a burden on social services. They're ripping off the government. They refuse to learn English."

Reyes cited reports that challenge these assertions. A study by the University of California showed that illegal immigrants use less health-care services per person than U.S. citizens do. Therefore, illegals do not place a disproportionate burden on California's health-care system. Further, Reyes noted, the Immigration Policy Center "recently reported that immigration increases gross domestic product by thirty-seven billion dollars a year. It found that immigrants pay more in taxes than they use in government services, and that the vast majority of immigrants are not eligible to receive public benefits." The Pew Research Center found that only 23 percent of first-generation Hispanic immigrants spoke English well. But 88 percent of the second generation spoke English well. This figure jumped to 94 percent for later generations. Finally, said Reyes, "A whopping 89 percent of Latinos believed that English is necessary for success in the USA."

slowly," Trimble said. And she believes those who think immigrants will move away are unrealistic. "It's happening all over the United States, so why would you think they're going to leave Austin?"

Gary Green is a professor of rural sociology at the University of Wisconsin–Madison. He noted that many historically white communities in the Midwest are faced with issues similar to Austin's.

> ❝ **There's no doubt that it's a threat to national identity, but studies suggest that immigration has a net positive economic impact on these towns, and probably socially as well.** ❞
>
> **—GARY GREEN,** UNIVERSITY OF WISCONSIN–MADISON
> PROFESSOR OF RURAL SOCIOLOGY
> **🌐 USA TODAY · AUGUST 29, 2008**

He said, "There's no doubt that it's a threat to national identity, but studies suggest that immigration has a net positive economic impact on these towns, and probably socially as well."

Such positive impact is evident in Austin. The city is home to fourteen Hispanic-owned businesses, including restaurants and stores that help make Main Street livelier than it's been in years. Some Hispanics are buying homes.

HEALTH CARE FOR IMMIGRANTS

The issue of benefits for illegal immigrants—especially health care—is a hot-button item on the agendas of communities across the country. Many people view health care as a benefit that undocumented people don't deserve and taxpayers can't afford. Other people view health care as a basic right for anyone who lives in the United States.

Data on health-care costs for illegal immigrants is rather sketchy. Hospitals and local health-care clinics don't typically ask about a patient's legal status because medical ethics (rules of professional conduct) frown on it. A 2004 study by the Federation for American Immigration Reform put California's annual cost of providing health care to illegal immigrants at $1.4 billion. Similar studies in Colorado and Minnesota yielded much smaller numbers: $31 million and $17 million, respectively.

Early in 2008, the comptroller (chief accounting officer)

of Texas estimated that illegal immigrants cost Texas hospitals $1.3 billion in 2006. Meanwhile, the University of Texas Medical Branch at Galveston considered denying cancer care to illegal immigrants.

Health-care costs have been rising rapidly across the country since the 1970s. Many states don't have enough money to cover these costs. They are looking for ways to cut health-care spending. For this reason, many state legislatures across the country are taking action to limit health-care spending for illegal immigrants.

For example, in May 2008, Oklahoma lawmakers banned illegal immigrants from receiving most public benefits, including health care. Other states, such as Nebraska, are considering similar laws. A bill introduced in Indiana in 2008 would require hospitals that receive public funds to report how much money they spend on caring for illegal immigrants.

Critics say laws that exclude illegal immigrants from publicly funded health care have many harmful consequences. The key problem: such laws make health workers into police officers. To avoid breaking the law, providers must ask about their patients' legal status. This in turn makes immigrants—both legal and illegal—afraid to seek health care. Illegal immigrants fear deportation. Legal immigrants often fear exposing undocumented family members. Avoiding preventive care (such as vaccinations) or treatment for illness can cause infectious diseases to spread among the general public. Avoiding nonemergency health care can also make small problems develop into big ones. When health problems become life-threatening, most people seek emergency care. Emergency care is much more expensive than routine health care.

LAW ENFORCEMENT

Cities such as Hazleton and states such as Oklahoma have enacted "get tough" immigration laws. But other local governments have chosen a different strategy.

Living under the Radar

Haya is a woman from the former Yugoslavia. Yugoslavia was made up of modern Slovenia, Croatia, Bosnia and Herzegovina, Serbia, Montenegro, Kosovo, and Macedonia. From 1991 to 2001, the region suffered a series of brutal wars that left widespread poverty, political turmoil, and ethnic hostility.

Haya, her husband, and their son together decided to start over in the United States. "I was the logical one to come first," Haya says. She speaks fluent English. Haya entered the United States on a tourist visa. She admits she had "every intention of staying."

In her home country, Haya was a teacher and school principal. In the United States, she can't use her education and experience. Doing so would expose her illegal status.

Haya cleans houses and serves as a home caregiver. She lives frugally and avoids exposure. She asks to be paid in cash. She fears the paper trail left by checks. A paper trail could lead immigration officials to Haya. She moves often, renting tiny rooms in rural Illinois towns. She finds work and lodging through church groups and employers. She has no car and no driver's license. She walks to work or asks others for rides. She worries about her health, because visiting a doctor would create a paper trail.

Haya's earnings are her family's main source of income. Her husband cannot find a job in their home country. Haya's family is saving money little by little, in hopes that they can reunite in the United States.

Haya's life as an illegal immigrant is hard. But she says it is better than the constant fear she left behind.

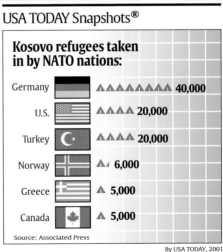

USA TODAY Snapshots®

Kosovo refugees taken in by NATO nations:

Germany	40,000
U.S.	20,000
Turkey	20,000
Norway	6,000
Greece	5,000
Canada	5,000

Source: Associated Press

By USA TODAY, 2001

Some U.S. cities have approved measures that limit local police enforcement of immigration law. In Detroit, Michigan, for example, a 2007 law says that police officers on duty may not ask anyone for a passport or other document to verify immigration status. Detroit's mayor, Ken Cockrel Jr., said his city has a growing Hispanic immigrant population. Cockrel told *USA TODAY* reporter Emily Bazar that city police should focus on protecting Detroiters, not on enforcing immigration law. He believes immigration law is a federal responsibility. Cockrel said simply, "I want Detroit police officers out there catching people who are stealing cars and mugging old ladies, not asking people for their passports."

San Francisco, California, passed its City and County of Refuge Ordinance in 1989. In 2007 Mayor Gavin Newsom reaffirmed the law by ordering city departments to develop formal procedures and training on the law. This law forbids city employees from helping ICE with investigations or arrests unless federal or state law or a warrant requires such help. City employees may not report the legal status of San Francisco residents to federal immigration agents when residents visit public health clinics, enroll their children in school, report crimes to the police, or seek other city services. The city says its law helps keep the community stable. It improves safety by making sure

Above: San Francisco mayor Gavin Newsom supports immigration-friendly city laws.

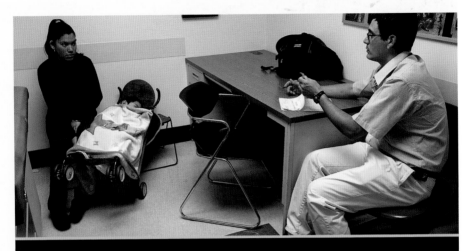

Above: An immigrant mother speaks with Dr. Neal Rojas of the Children's Health Center in San Francisco, California. In some U.S. cities, such as San Francisco, illegal immigrants can use community services without fear of arrest or deportation. These cities are called sanctuary cities.

all residents feel comfortable calling during emergencies. It keeps families and workers healthy by providing safe access to schools, clinics, and other services.

The National Immigration Law Center (NILC), an agency that protects and promotes the rights of low-income immigrants and their families, supports city laws like Detroit's and San Francisco's. NILC spokesperson Joan Friedland said these policies promote public safety. They make immigrants more willing to cooperate with police and other officials. "If people fear the police at every turn," Friedland said, "that undermines community policing, which undermines community safety."

On the other hand, many state and federal lawmakers are concerned about policies such as those in Detroit and San Francisco. They believe these policies not only break the law but also encourage illegal immigration. Opponents have labeled places with such laws "sanctuary cities"—or places where illegal immigrants are free of the law.

Lawmakers seek 'sanctuary cities' crackdown; Bills target havens of illegal immigrants

From the Pages of USA TODAY STATE AND FEDERAL lawmakers are calling for tough action against "sanctuary cities," reflecting a backlash against communities that they say break the law and encourage illegal immigration.

At least three states are considering taking the path of Colorado, which adopted an anti-sanctuary law last year. It denies some funding to communities that prevent police and other municipal employees from cooperating with immigration authorities. Similar measures are pending in Michigan, New Jersey and Wisconsin.

Nationally, members of Congress are proposing federal legislation and presidential candidates are urging sanctions.

Local law enforcement officers come into contact with immigrants every day, says Michigan state Rep. Kim Meltzer, a Republican. "Why should they be restricted, have their hands tied?" she asks.

Her bill would forbid local governments from telling police and other government employees not to cooperate with federal authorities and would require police to report people they arrest who are suspected illegal immigrants.

In May, the Detroit City Council unanimously approved an ordinance [law] that, among other things, forbids city officials from asking the immigration status of people not suspected of crimes.

Council President Ken Cockrel Jr. says the city has a growing Hispanic immigrant population and is home to large Middle Eastern communities. Local police should focus on protecting them, he says, not enforcing immigration law, which is a federal responsibility.

"I want Detroit police officers out there catching people who are stealing cars and mugging old ladies, not asking people for their passports," he says.

Detroit's ordinance is among at least 82 policies nationwide that limit the enforcement of immigration laws by state and local authorities, according to the National Immigration Law Center. The policies promote public safety by making immigrants more willing to cooperate with police and other officials, says the group's Joan Friedland.

"If people fear the police at every turn, that undermines community policing, which undermines community safety," she says.

Mitt Romney and Fred Thompson are among Republican presidential candidates who counter that sanctuary policies encourage law-breaking by shielding illegal immigrants. They propose that some federal funding be denied to cities that have them.

Florida Republican Rep. Ginny Brown-Waite has introduced one of the anti-sanctuary measures in Congress. Her bill would revoke some Homeland Security funds from sanctuary cities.

"The public is speaking loud and clear that they don't want . . . their elected officials allowing illegals to move into the area and use services from the area," she says.

In Wisconsin, Republican state Sen. Glenn Grothman plans to introduce a measure next week that forbids cities and counties from adopting sanctuary policies.

New Jersey state Sen. Nicholas Asselta, a Republican, says he'll introduce a measure next month.

—Emily Bazar

Opponents are calling for tough federal action against such cities. Lawmakers such as Republican Kim Meltzer, a Michigan state senator, would like to see federal laws and penalties against sanctuary cities. Meltzer noted that local police officers have daily contact with immigrants. "Why should they be restricted, have their hands tied?" she asked. Meltzer has proposed a law forbidding local governments from telling their employees not to cooperate with federal immigration officials. The proposed law would also require local police to report to ICE arrestees who may be illegal immigrants.

Former Massachusetts governor Mitt Romney and former Tennessee senator Fred Thompson agree with Meltzer. Both believe sanctuary cities shield illegal immigrants

Above: Immigration opponents do not like that laws in some cities keep local police from reporting illegal immigrants to federal immigration agencies. A proposed law would impose a federal standard to change this policy.

Above: ICE officials oversee the deportation of illegal immigrants in Texas. A proposed federal law would enable both ICE and local police to work together to curb illegal immigration.

and encourage lawbreaking. Romney and Thompson separately proposed denying federal funding to such cities.

Ginny Brown-Waite, a Republican representative from Florida, introduced one of several anti-sanctuary bills in the U.S. Congress in 2007. Her bill would punish sanctuary cities by yanking some of their Homeland Security funds. Brown-Waite said, "The public is speaking loud and clear that they don't want . . . their elected officials allowing illegals to move into the area and use services from the area."

CHAPTER FOUR

Fences, Raids, and Harsh Measures

A 2006 *USA TODAY* EDITORIAL CITED A RECENT POLL of U.S. public opinion on immigration. The poll found that "nine of every ten Americans say immigration is a serious problem, and three-fourths want more done to keep illegal immigrants out."

In response to the passionate immigration debate swirling across the country, the U.S. government and some local governments have beefed up security. Security measures include providing more money and staff for the Border Patrol. They also include extending the fence along the United States–Mexico border. This border sees the most illegal entries into the United States.

In addition, Immigration and Customs Enforcement has increased raids of workplaces that employ large numbers of illegal immigrants. In these raids, agents arrest and often deport any illegal workers they find. Harsh local laws meant to drive out illegal immigrants are another part of the effort to increase U.S. security.

Left: A metal fence extends into the Pacific Ocean. It separates Mexico from the United States between the cities of Tijuana, Mexico, and San Diego, California.

BEEFED-UP BORDER PATROL

When the 1996 immigration bill (IIRIRA) passed, it provided funds to double the Border Patrol from five thousand to ten thousand agents by 2001. In 2006 the force was twelve thousand strong. In 2008 about seventeen thousand agents patrolled U.S. borders.

Above: In 2009 President Barack Obama appointed Janet Napolitano as the third secretary of the Department of Homeland Security. Partly in response to increased drug violence and poverty along the Mexican border, Napolitano has increased the number of U.S. agents patrolling the border.

In March 2009, Department of Homeland Security secretary Janet Napolitano announced a plan to send 360 additional agents to the U.S.–Mexico border. This plan is meant to not only stop illegal drugs and immigrants from entering the United States but also to stop the outward flow of illegal weapons and cash into Mexico.

The border city of Laredo, Texas, calls itself the gateway to Mexico. Northbound traffic in the area suggests that Laredo is also one of the main gateways into the United States. Laredo's Border Patrol caught nearly seventy-five thousand illegal immigrants in 2006. During the spring of 2007, the force stopped more than fifteen thousand.

These numbers put local agents on the front lines of the immigration debate. Laredo's Border Patrol force consists largely of Mexican American U.S. citizens.

> ❝ **I'm a U.S. citizen, and I swore to uphold the laws of this country.** ❞
>
> —**GINO RODRIGUEZ,** U.S. BORDER PATROL AGENT
>
> ◉ **USA TODAY · MAY 8, 2007**

Many of the agents are bilingual, speaking both English and Spanish fluently.

One agent is Gino Rodriguez, the son of Mexican immigrants. He calls himself "an American of Mexican heritage." A member of the Border Patrol for nearly twenty years, Rodriguez has turned away thousands of people trying to enter the United States from Mexico.

Over and over again, Rodriguez has seen immigrants

Above: Border patrol agents can watch activity along the U.S.-Mexico border on TV monitors. Video cameras on private land surrounding Harlingen, Texas, help agents spot immigrants trying to sneak across the border illegally.

"on the verge of death," stranded by smugglers in midsummer, when temperatures top 100°F (38°C). In Spanish they plead to him for mercy. He shook his head, as if in answer to the immigrants. He said, "I understand their plight like any human being would." He adds that his job "isn't just about catching people, it's about saving lives, too." His agency has a special rescue team that treats immigrants in medical distress. But in the end, Rodriguez said, "I'm a U.S. citizen, and I swore to uphold the laws of this country."

THE FENCE

The DHS is eager to complete 670 miles (1,078 km) of fencing along the 1,969-mile (3,169 km) U.S.–Mexico border. DHS is hopeful that the fence will dramatically curb illegal immigration. As of January 2009, 580 miles (933 km) were complete. The idea of a border fence pleases hardcore immigration foes. But the fence itself has created heated opposition.

In April 2008, DHS used its legal authority to waive environmental and land management laws. These laws are meant to protect wildlife, private land, and human artifacts (historical objects such as tools or structures). But following these laws would have slowed down the fence construction. Former DHS secretary Michael Chertoff explained, "Criminal activity at the border does not stop for endless debate or protracted litigation [lengthy lawsuits]. The waivers will enable important security projects to keep moving forward." The department promised that it "remains deeply committed to environmental responsibility" and that it will make every effort to "ensure impacts to the environment, wildlife and cultural and historic artifacts are analyzed and minimized."

DHS's move created a firestorm of protest—both in Washington and along the border. House Homeland Security Committee chairman Bennie Thompson said, "[The] waiver represents an extreme abuse of authority. Waiver authority should only be used as a last resort." Landowners, ranchers, and environmentalists along the border objected too. Some didn't want their land taken for the fence. Others didn't want important plants and wildlife to be disturbed.

The fence project has sparked especially fierce opposition in Texas. This project would damage the Lower Rio Grande Valley National Wildlife Refuge. Bulldozers would clear 500 acres (202 hectares) of land in the refuge. Then workers would build a 16-foot (5-meter) fence along the Rio Grande. This fence would block river access for many animals on the U.S. side, depriving them of water and food. The refuge is a popular destination in Texas for ecotourists. Ecotourism pumps about $125 million per year into the

Above: Border patrol agent Eugenio (Gino) Rodriguez discovers discarded clothing and shoes in the weeds alongside the Rio Grande in Texas. A proposal is in the works to build a fence in this heavily guarded stretch along the U.S.–Mexico border.

local economy. With the refuge carved up and its animals suffering, Texans worry that their state will lose badly needed tourism dollars.

In addition, the 153-mile (246 km) fence would slice through the University of Texas in Brownsville. Part of the campus would end up in Mexico. So would historic Fort Brown and the district office of State Representative Ryan Guillen.

The Texas Border Coalition condemns the fence. This coalition consists of mayors, county judges, economic development experts, and Texas governor Rick Perry. Perry commented, "If you build a 30-foot [9 m] wall or fence, the 32-foot [10 m] ladder business is going to get real good."

In August 2008, U.S. Customs and Border Protection began building a 3.5-mile (5.6 km) section of fence near San Diego, California. The fence runs through a deep canyon called Smuggler's Gulch. Before a 1990s crackdown, Smuggler's Gulch was a major route for illegal immigration into the

Above: A crew installs new sections of fence along the Mexican border near Calexico, California. This particular project had contractors installing 8 miles (13 km) of fence 15 feet (4.6 m) high.

USA TODAY Snapshots®

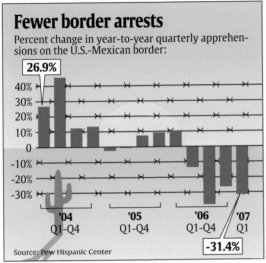

Fewer border arrests

Percent change in year-to-year quarterly apprehensions on the U.S.-Mexican border:

26.9%

Source: Pew Hispanic Center

-31.4%

By Adrienne Lewis, USA TODAY, 2007

The fence construction followed twelve years of planning, environmental reviews, and legal challenges. Because this section of fence requires filling a deep canyon, the project costs about fifty-seven million dollars. That's about sixteen million dollars per mile (1.6 km). The rest of the border fence costs about two million to three million dollars per mile.

"It's crazy," said Victor Clark Alfaro, director of the Binational Center for Human Rights in Tijuana, Mexico. "I don't see the justification to spend $60 million on an area that's no longer an important crossing." He predicted that the new fence would cut illegal crossings in the San Diego area to "almost zero" but would also seriously damage the environment. He doesn't believe the results will be worth the financial and environmental cost.

United States. Hundreds—sometimes thousands—of immigrants per day traveled through the canyon.

Illegal crossings here have dropped a lot since the crackdown. Border Patrol spokesman Alex Renteria said arrests in this area totaled 16,738 between October 2007 and July 2008. That's about 60 per day. Mike Fisher, chief of the San Diego Border Patrol, believes the fence is necessary despite the decreased traffic. He explained that "it's still a vulnerability [weakness] that's being exploited [taken advantage of] today."

Like Perry and Alfaro, many U.S. citizens feel the U.S.–Mexico border fencing is a ridiculous effort. They believe it will do little to stop illegal crossings. Border Patrol agent Ramiro Cordero confirmed that a fence can only slow down determined immigrants. He said the new fence between El Paso, Texas, and Ciudad Juarez, Mexico, "will not stop people from digging underneath it, driving around it or cutting through it with a blowtorch."

Immigration routes shift as the areas of U.S. border enforcement shift. A veteran Border Patrol agent showed author Luis Alberto Urrea a portion of the Arizona–Mexico border slated for a new fence. "Just east of where we stood," observed Urrea, "the fence will stop. There are big scary mountains… included in the plan as natural immigration barriers. These are the same mountains over which many of the undocumented are already walking to avoid the good men and women of the U.S. Border Patrol."

Many critics fear that border fences will damage families and societies in the region. The mayor of Brownsville said, "[The fences] are going to kill our communities along the border. The rest of America has no idea how we live our lives here. We are linked by the Rio Grande, not divided by it." El Paso county attorney Jose Rodriguez agrees: "It does violence to our sense of

> **" [The fences] are going to kill our communities along the border. The rest of America has no idea how we live our lives here. We are linked by the Rio Grande, not divided by it. "**
>
> **—PAT AHUMADA,**
> MAYOR OF BROWNSVILLE, TEXAS, 2008

community. For 400 years, people have been going back and forth across the river." Ruben Alvarado, an El Paso resident whose mother and sister live in Juarez, said, "To me, Juarez and El Paso are the same city."

Opponents of border fencing believe it's not only useless and destructive but also a cop-out. They say it's a sign of two countries' unwillingness to address the economic problems underlying illegal immigration. A *San Francisco Chronicle* reader wrote, "Do we believe that this expensive, destructive fence is going to fix the problem of [immigrants] needing to feed their families . . . and employers in this country trying to find workers . . . ? We need to figure out why people are coming here (we employ them!), not assume that a big, expensive fence is going to keep desperate economic refugees out."

Yet support for the fence remains strong at the federal level. Some local residents and officials support fencing too. In urban areas, where most of the border is under video surveillance, agents can spot people trying to climb or cut the fence. It gives agents a few extra seconds to catch illegal immigrants before they disappear into the city. Cordero says, "It makes the job a lot easier when you have that fence." El Paso resident Oscar Davila says the new fence makes him feel safer from the drug-related violence in Juarez.

RAIDS AND ROUNDUPS

Workplace raids are another tactic federal authorities use to deal with illegal immigration. Before a raid, ICE collects evidence showing that many employees at a given worksite are undocumented. ICE uses this evidence to get a search warrant so it can conduct a raid.

In a typical raid, armed agents surround the worksite. Agents demand that no one leave the site without ICE's permission. Agents move employees to contained areas for questioning. If employees do not have their immigration documents on hand, company staff can retrieve copies from

Above: Residents in Marshalltown, Iowa, look on as ICE officers conduct a raid on the Swift meatpacking plant there.

company files. Or employees can contact family to bring documents to the worksite. While some agents conduct questioning, other agents search the site and seize documents, computer equipment, and other evidence. ICE agents arrest employees who cannot prove their legal status. ICE takes the arrestees to various detention centers.

Officials say raids have netted thousands of illegal immigrants. In December 2006, for example, ICE officers raided Swift meatpacking plants in

The Ripple Effects of Raids

Perry, Iowa, is a town of seventy-six hundred people about 200 miles (322 km) southwest of Postville. Like Postville, Perry has seen an increase in its Hispanic population. Jobs at a Tyson meatpacking plant on the outskirts of Perry have attracted many of these new residents. With about twelve hundred workers, the plant is Perry's largest employer.

The ICE raid in Postville sparked rumors in Perry. Many people thought that Perry would be the ICE's next target. Soon after hearing about Postville, Mayor Viivi Shirley met with Tyson's plant manager. She confirmed that Tyson was hiring workers legally. But Shirley still worried about a raid in Perry. Shirley said she was "proud of the way newer Hispanic residents have melded with Perry's older, mostly Caucasian residents." She feared a raid "would undo years of progress."

The rumors turned out to be false. But it left the town's Hispanic population (about one-quarter of the total) pondering a new and harsh small-town reality.

"These raids have really highlighted the difficulties towns face in this situation," said Ana-Maria Garcia Wahl. A sociology professor at Wake Forest University in North Carolina, Wahl studies immigration issues in the Midwest and South. She noted, "I'm not sure all of these towns have an ability to cope and provide the crisis intervention" needed after workplace raids.

Nebraska and five other states. Arrests in these raids totaled 1,297 people.

ICE officers raided the Agriprocessors meatpacking plant in Postville, Iowa, on May 12, 2008. Postville is a town of about 2,300 people. ICE agents arrested 389 workers. Federal prosecutors billed the raid as "the largest criminal worksite enforcement ever in the United States."

On August 25, 2008, ICE agents raided the Howard Industries manufacturing plant in Laurel, Mississippi. They detained 595 workers. Federal officials said a tip

Above: An illlegal immigrant rounded up in a workplace raid at a Chinese restaurant in Iowa is handcuffed and arrested.

that most illegal immigrants enter the United States because plenty of companies are willing to hire them. Worksites with large numbers of illegal workers often know that their workforces are on shaky legal ground. Some companies actually seek out the cheap labor that illegal immigrants provide. Other employers fail to check their workers' status carefully. Yet the effort ICE spent arresting, jailing, and deporting illegal immigrants dwarfed its corporate enforcement effort.

from a union worker "several years ago" led them to investigate the plant. One immigrant caught in the raid said fellow workers applauded during the roundup.

Critics of ICE's ramped-up roundups from 2006 to 2008 say they've been destructive, costly, and largely ineffective. ICE's strategy seemed to ignore

In addition, ICE's strategy "has instilled fear in towns across the country." Many folks throughout the United States dread going to work. The raids create hard feelings in communities with immigrant populations. City leaders worry that years of work bringing their constituents together might go up in smoke.

Above: A young girl holds a sign during an immigrant rights rally in Los Angeles, California. Children of illegal immigrants are often orphaned when their parents get caught and deported.

Workplace raids trouble some Americans for humanitarian reasons. Christopher Nugent, a Washington immigration attorney, said ICE routinely separated families, forcing detained and deported parents to leave their children with friends or relatives. "This is the hidden underbelly of immigration enforcement," said Nugent. The welfare of children affected by immigration raids became a bigger issue as the scope of the raids grew.

In an August 8, 2008, *USA TODAY* column, Raul Reyes called the ICE raids "government-sanctioned racial profiling." Racial profiling is using racial or ethnic traits to determine whether someone is likely to commit a certain crime. The Fourth Amendment to the U.S. Constitution forbids unreasonable search and seizure without probable cause. Probable cause does not include belonging to a race that an official believes is more likely to commit a crime, because most people of all races are law-abiding.

After deportation, migrants determined to return

From the Pages of USA TODAY

SANTA TECLA, El Salvador—When Oscar Ordooez, 56, pleaded guilty to attempted theft in Colorado, he didn't realize he could lose his right to live in the USA. Now he sits on his sister's balcony overlooking the green Salvadoran hills, dreaming of the life he left behind and plotting his illegal return.

Pedro Berrios, 25, reads to his 5-year-old son in their cinder-block home next to the filthy Tomayate River. Berrios will keep trying to enter the USA illegally, he says, because "I don't see another way out of here."

The lives of Ordooez and Berrios converged on Feb. 28 when they boarded a plane in Texas with 117 other men and women. They were being deported to El Salvador, targets of the U.S. government's crackdown on illegal immigrants.

The government ramped up deportations after 9/11 as part of a broad effort to secure U.S. borders. Yet, as the Salvadorans' stories show, the policy is up against the economic reality of life in developing countries. The two say they went to the USA to escape poverty and crime. Now that the deportation flight has left them back in their homeland, they say the same things may spur them to try again.

"I don't want to stay here," Ordooez says. "In the U.S., you have a chance to work and buy whatever you need."

Ordooez, who lived in the USA more than 18 years, isn't giving up. "My life is not here," he says of El Salvador. "My life is there."

Ordooez finished the sixth grade and started working at age 12. In his early 30s, he went to the USA for the first time and was caught three days later, kicking off a cycle of illegal entries and run-ins with the Border Patrol. He says he was sent home 18 times, but government records show he was officially deported just once.

What tenacity [determination] couldn't do for him, marriage did. Ordooez met Jean Gibson, an American who helped Salvadorans fleeing civil war. When he returned to El Salvador in 1987, she followed and they married. He got a waiver to immigrate the next year and became a legal permanent resident.

His immigration troubles began not when the couple divorced in 1994 but when he was convicted of a felony in Colorado.

Ordooez was working as a janitor at a Cripple Creek casino. In 1996, his landlords accused him of stealing two rings and other items. He says he didn't steal the jewelry but that his landlady gave it to him to sell. Acting on what he says was bad advice from a public defender who didn't advise him of the consequences to his immigration status, Ordooez pleaded guilty in 2002 to attempted theft.

An attorney helped Ordooez get the case dismissed and the felony erased from his record in 2005, but it was too late. He lost his legal status and returned to El Salvador to live with his sister in Santa Tecla.

He didn't stay long. Last year, he was caught twice trying to cross the border. He spent four months in jail. Despite the threat of a longer sentence if he's caught again, he says he'll return. He wants to earn money for his family in Santa Tecla.

"I don't have a choice," Ordooez says. "Right now, I don't have a life in this country."

Berrios says he has mounting debts. Because visas are too difficult to get, he says, he'll keep trying to sneak into the USA.

A construction worker . . . , Berrios can make $20 a day, but sometimes he goes months without work.

"Look at the reality of our house and how we live," he says of his crime-infested neighborhood and unfinished home, which overlooks a river whose polluted water runs purple, red and brown. When family members go to the grocery, he says, they run to minimize chances of being robbed.

For now, the home's windows are boarded with plywood, and the walls and floors are bare, but Berrios says he dreams of making it a beautiful sanctuary for his family.

In January, his mother took a $7,000 mortgage on her house to finance his trip to join four brothers and a sister in the San Francisco Bay Area. He was caught in Texas. "I'll try again because I have no other way to pay back the money," he says through a translator.

Berrios says he doesn't want to stay in the USA. He wants to earn money for his family and return to El Salvador to open a business. He's unapologetic about his plans. He says people like him just want to give their families a chance to rise out of poverty. . . . "That's what's motivating me to try to cross again."

—Emily Bazar

Reyes suggested that comprehensive immigration reform is the only way to halt such abuses. Reyes acknowledged that the United States "has every right to deport illegal aliens.... But the government has been charging them with identity theft and sentencing them to serve jail time first."

In April 2009, the Obama administration announced reforms to its workplace raid procedures. DHS issued new guidelines to all local ICE offices. These guidelines instruct agents to pursue evidence against employers who knowingly hire illegal workers before going after the workers.

"Enforcement efforts focused on employers better target the root causes of illegal immigration," the guidelines say. "Employers who knowingly hire illegal workers ... are not sufficiently punished or deterred by the arrest of their illegal workforce."

The new guidelines also require agents raiding workplaces with at least twenty-five

---

Sent back

The United States deported 282,548 illegal immigrants in 2007. The top 10 countries:

Mexico **136,069**
Honduras **29,273**
Guatemala **24,765**
El Salvador **19,862**
Brazil **2,949**
Dominican Republic **2,721**
Colombia **2,598**
Nicaragua **2,240**
Ecuador **1,371**
Haiti **1,244**

Source: Immigration and Customs Enforcement

By Adrienne Lewis, USA TODAY, 2008

> **" In the USA, all people deserve to be treated humanely—and with justice. "**
>
> **—RAUL REYES,** USA TODAY COLUMNIST
> USA TODAY · AUGUST 8, 2008

The Problem with 1804

Oklahoma's neighbors have mixed feelings about 1804. Daniel Kowalski, a Texas immigration lawyer, believes such a law would never pass in Texas because about 16 percent of Texans are foreign-born and would not support restrictions against immigrants. Arkansas, on the other hand—with fewer foreign-born residents—seems ready to follow in Oklahoma's footsteps. Arkansans resent the influx of people from Oklahoma fleeing 1804. Arkansas lawmakers may introduce an 1804-like bill in 2009. "We're getting a lot of pressure at home," said Arkansas state representative Rick Green, because Arkansans "see what Oklahoma's done" and want to do the same.

employees to follow humanitarian rules. This means that agents can release detainees who are sick or who are sole caregivers for small children.

HARSH LAWS

Congressional efforts to overhaul U.S. immigration collapsed in 2007. Afterward, harsh local laws targeting illegal immigrants passed in Oklahoma, Arizona, Colorado, Georgia, and other states with large immigrant populations. Such laws raise the threat of workplace raids. In response to the laws, many illegal immigrants returned to their home countries. Others moved to neighboring states where laws are less strict.

One of these new laws is the Oklahoma Taxpayer and Citizen Protection Act of 2007. The law began as House Bill 1804, so many Oklahomans simply call it 1804. It is a sweeping law. It suspends or revokes (takes away) business licenses of employers who knowingly hire illegal immigrants. It makes transporting or sheltering illegal immigrants a felony (serious crime). It also denies driver's licenses and public benefits, such as money for rent and fuel, to illegal immigrants.

Even before the bill took effect in November 2007, businesses and workers were suffering its consequences. Every autumn, workers at the 600-acre (243-hectare) Greenleaf Nursery southeast of Tulsa prepare for deadly winter frosts. They ship plants, build greenhouses, and bunch trees to protect them from the cold. But by late October 2007, about forty immigrant employees had simply disappeared. "Some went to Texas, some went to Arkansas," said nursery president Randy Davis. "They just left." Asked why his workers fled, Davis replied, "Those states don't have 1804."

By early 2008, fifteen thousand to twenty thousand illegal immigrants had left Tulsa County alone, according to the Greater Tulsa Hispanic Chamber of Commerce. "People are leaving to Mexico or Canada or other states," said Jim Garcia, manager of a Tulsa grocery store. While the law has been successful in forcing illegal immigrants to leave, these departures can harm a company's profits. Garcia said his sales fell by 40 percent between November 2007 and January 2008. During the same period, Chris Ellison lost eight of sixteen workers. Ellison runs a cotton gin in Hollis, Oklahoma. When some workers left, those remaining had to work overtime. This sent Ellison's payroll costs soaring.

Another 1804 provision requires employers with government contracts to more thoroughly check the histories of new employees. Employers must check a federal database to see if new hires are legally eligible to work. If the employers don't do so, they may lose their contracts.

Tim Wagner is an owner of a Mexican restaurant in Oklahoma City. "I've already had customers who came in here and told me they've fired employees because they didn't know if they were here legally," he said.

Some business owners and lawmakers fear 1804 will hit consumers where it hurts. They argue that a smaller pool of workers for certain jobs

Above: Field-workers help load iceberg lettuce into boxes in Bakersfield, California. Illegal migrant workers often do seasonal work in the United States. Many U.S. employers say they have trouble hiring citizens for such work.

will cause delays in producing goods. Employers will also have to compete more fiercely for workers. This will lead to higher wages and thus to higher prices. Republican state representative Shane Jett, who opposed 1804, said bluntly that without changes, the law will be Oklahoma's "single most destructive economic disaster since the Dust Bowl," a prolonged drought that hit the Great Plains during the Great Depression of the 1930s.

State Representative Randy Terrill, the Republican author of 1804, says the bill will save money. He says taxpayers won't be paying for services to illegal immigrants. "There's significant evidence that ... 1804 is achieving its intended purpose, which is illegal aliens leaving the state of Oklahoma," he said. "1804 is a model not only for Oklahoma, but for other states and the nation as well." Terrill has little sympathy for employers who hire illegal workers. He believes

> " **I would love to hire twenty U.S. citizens here [but] local people are not going to quit a job to work three weeks during the year.** "

—CHRIS ELLISON,
EMPLOYER OF MOTLEY GIN, INC., HOLLIS, OKLAHOMA
USA TODAY · JANUARY 10, 2008

1804 will create jobs for U.S. citizens.

However, some employers say it's hard to hire legal workers in their industries. For example, Chris Ellison of Motley Gin in Hollis hires workers for short periods of time. During the cotton harvest, his factory processes raw cotton. Ellison says, "I would love to hire twenty U.S. citizens here [but] local people are not going to quit a job to work three weeks during the year."

Colorado has also passed strict immigration laws. One provision gives employers

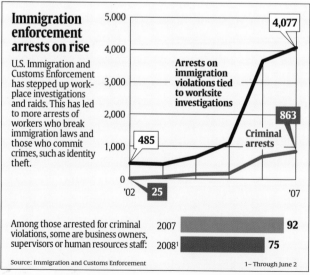

Immigration enforcement arrests on rise

U.S. Immigration and Customs Enforcement has stepped up workplace investigations and raids. This has led to more arrests of workers who break immigration laws and those who commit crimes, such as identity theft.

Arrests on immigration violations tied to worksite investigations — 4,077

Criminal arrests — 863

485

'02   25   '07

Among those arrested for criminal violations, some are business owners, supervisors or human resources staff:
2007 — 92
2008[1] — 75

Source: Immigration and Customs Enforcement
1– Through June 2

By Julie Snider, USA TODAY, 2008

twenty days to verify the legal status of new hires. Employers do so by checking and photocopying official documents such as driver's licenses and Social Security cards. Colorado state senator Dave Schultheis said he'd heard that illegal immigrants were leaving. "It's absolutely a good thing," he said. "We want to make Colorado the least friendly state to people who are here illegally."

Immigrants are moving away from Hazleton, Pennsylvania, too. Even though a federal court struck down Hazleton's Illegal Immigrant Relief Act, people are still leaving. Rudy Espinal, head of the Hazleton Hispanic Business Association, said, "Some people have told me that they're leaving because they don't want their kids to grow up in [a hostile] environment like this." Hazleton mayor Lou Barletta responded, "We don't want to chase immigrants away, just the illegal aliens who are causing many of the problems we are having."

CHAPTER FIVE

Immigrants and the U.S. Economy

THE U.S. CENSUS BUREAU'S 2008 FIGURES PROJECT A population surge. The total U.S. population will grow from three hundred million to four hundred million in thirty-one years. According to Mark Mather, who studies demographic trends for the nonpartisan Population Reference Bureau, this surge "affects quality of life in very important ways. We're already experiencing that in traffic congestion, in schools and in our crowded coastal areas."

Immigration foes say immigrants are unwelcome competitors for scarce resources. Opponents claim that immigration damages the U.S. economy. Immigrants hog U.S. jobs, drain public resources, and boost the nation's crime rate.

Immigration advocates object. They say that immigrants affect the U.S. economy positively by filling unmet labor needs. They pay taxes and buy goods and services. These contributions outweigh the few public services they use. Advocates also say studies refute the

Left: Kindergarten teacher Bret Bell works with his class in a portable classroom in Spring Hill, Tennessee. From 2000 to 2008, the town's population has tripled. Many U.S. communities are growing as immigrants join them.

claim that immigrants are more likely to commit crimes.

IMMIGRANTS AND JOBS

For decades, nativist Americans have argued that immigrants take jobs from U.S. workers. Other people respond that immigrants fill jobs that many Americans don't want. Furthermore, immigrants expand the nation's economy by paying taxes and buying food, housing, and other goods and services.

Evidence suggests that immigrants do not threaten the workforce. In fact, scholars say, the U.S. economy will need immigrants to fill future jobs. A 2005 Immigration Policy Center study found that immigrants will be "critical to filling future labor gaps." According to that study, seventy-six million baby boomers (Americans born between 1946 and 1964) will retire by 2030. Meanwhile, only forty-six million native-born workers will enter the U.S. workforce. That leaves a shortage of at least thirty million workers.

The U.S. Bureau of Labor Statistics (BLS) projects that between 2002 and 2012, the number of U.S. jobs will increase by twenty-one million for a total of fifty-six million. According to BLS, many of the new jobs will be in areas that require few skills. Therefore, these jobs will not pay high wages. They will be unsuitable for older and better-educated U.S. workers. Thus, "many immigrants with their younger age profile and lower education levels will be needed to fill these jobs."

In the short term, however, all U.S. workers—legal and illegal—are facing a troubled economy. Amilcar Guzman, for example, came to the United States from El Salvador in 1999, when he was eighteen years old. He ended up in Manassas, Virginia. The housing industry was booming at that time. He quickly found high-paying jobs cutting lumber, driving nails, and operating construction vehicles. He bought a car and got married. The housing boom drew thousands of job seekers just like him from Latin America. But in late 2005, the boom began to go bust. It happened little by little, month by month. Contractors stopped hiring. Guzman found himself unemployed.

"There's no work here anymore," he said. "And when there's no work, it's time for Latinos to go back to the countries where they came from." Guzman gathered his family, boarded a plane, and headed back to El Salvador. He planned to open an auto repair shop with the money he'd saved.

Indeed, many immigrants are returning to their home countries. A recent study by the Pew Hispanic Center, a nonpartisan research group, shows illegal immigration slowing. From 2000 to 2005, about eight hundred thousand illegal immigrants entered the United States each year. Since 2005 that number has been about five hundred thousand per year. The number of illegal entries has dipped below the number of legal entries for the first time in a decade.

Above: Rosario Araujo *(left)* and José Zavala *(right)* returned home to Mexico in October 2008. The couple had been living illegally in Gilbert, Arizona, but returned to Mexico because they couldn't find enough work.

www.usatoday.com

News
SECTION A

February 11, 2008

In Mexico, an energized economy raises hopes

From the Pages of
USA TODAY

IXMIQUILPAN, Mexico—As Mexicans risk their lives to illegally immigrate to the USA and shootouts among drug lords dominate the news, it's understandable why Mexico might be perceived as a place with little hope.

Yet many Mexicans say their future looks brighter than it has in generations.

The economy is growing, and poverty rates are declining. Crime is down, public health and education levels are improving, and Mexico's democracy is more robust than at any time in its history.

As the debate over illegal immigration percolates in the USA, there are hopes on both sides of the border that Mexico's improving economy eventually will provide enough jobs to encourage significant numbers of Mexicans to stay and prosper in their country.

Such displays of optimism were uncommon a decade ago, when Mexico was reeling from an economic meltdown and an armed uprising in the southern state of Chiapas. Banks collapsed nationwide under a mountain of unpaid loans.

Politically, Mexico was monopolized [controlled] by the Institutional Revolutionary Party (PRI), which had used payoffs, intimidation and election fraud to rule the nation under a virtual one-party system since 1929.

But change was in the air.

The 1994 North American Free Trade Agreement opened a huge market for Mexican-made goods, spurring the construction of factories along the U.S. border.

Meanwhile, a new generation of government technocrats, many of them Ivy League [prestigious U.S. university] graduates, began to tame the runaway public spending and inflation that had locked the Mexican economy in bust-and-boom cycles for generations.

In 2000, the conservative Vicente Fox became the first president from outside the PRI in seven decades. Under Fox and his successor,

Felipe Calderon, inflation has averaged about 4% a year with no major financial meltdowns.

"The stability of the past decade-plus has allowed financial markets and banks to grow up. Mortgages exist now. People can get loans. There has been a birth of a middle class in Mexico," says Gray Newman, head economist for Latin America at Morgan Stanley investment bank in New York.

Economic growth has been modest, averaging about 3% per year, but the greatest improvement in living standards among Mexico's 103 million people has been seen among those of humble means—surprising, perhaps, given the historic gap between rich and poor.

Mexico's economy created roughly 950,000 jobs last year, according to the government.

That is a major improvement from a decade ago, when job growth was nearly flat, but still not quite enough to absorb the 1.1 million Mexicans who entered the workforce in 2007.

That disparity, plus the fact U.S. jobs often pay five times as much as those in Mexico, is a major reason why migrants continue crossing into the USA, Newman says.

However, if Mexico's economy keeps growing at similar or slightly better rates, and if population growth continues to level out [as it has in recent years], then within a generation there might not be enough working-age people to fill its labor force, says Leonardo Martinez-Diaz, a Mexico specialist at the Brookings Institution, a Washington-based think tank.

Mexico "could go over the next 20 years from being an exporter of people to an importer of people," Martinez-Diaz says. "That would be a pretty remarkable change."

Such good news, though, has been overshadowed by the drug war in cities along the U.S. border.

Beheadings, shootouts in daylight and a wave of police killings have convinced many Mexicans their country is not safe.

"The middle class has grown, and the political situation is a little better," says Cesar Sumano, whose wife was carjacked outside a grocery store last year.

"But it's still a hard country to live in. We've got a long way to go."

—Chris Hawley

The report does not give reasons for the decline. Jeffrey Passel with the Pew Hispanic Center and other experts point to a slowing U.S. economy. They also point to tougher enforcement—especially ICE raids. ICE sent nearly 340,000 illegal immigrants home from October 2007 through September 2008.

William Frey is a demographer at the Brookings Institution, a centrist think tank. He cautions against crediting harsher enforcement for the drop in illegal immigration. He says illegals are leaving and fewer are coming because jobs are vanishing in the United States. "Illegal immigrants follow the networks of their friends and families," Frey said. "They hear about jobs drying up, and they decide this isn't the time to come."

IMMIGRANTS AND EDUCATION

Immigrants are feeling the crunch not only in employment opportunities but also in opportunities for higher education. Since 2006 Arizona, Colorado, Georgia, and Oklahoma have changed certain rules about paying for higher education. These states have refused lower, in-state tuition rates to students who entered the United States illegally with their parents but grew up in these states. That's a reversal from earlier in the decade, when ten states passed laws allowing in-state rates for such students. In addition, a 2008 Georgia law prevents illegal immigrants from receiving state scholarships and certain student loans.

In the summer of 2008, South Carolina became the first state to bar undocumented students from all public colleges and universities. At the same time, all fifty-eight of North Carolina's community colleges stopped enrolling illegal immigrants. That action came after the state's attorney general (chief law-enforcement official) said admitting such students might break federal law.

William Gheen of Americans for Legal Immigration said, "The new trend is to kick illegal aliens out of college altogether." The group opposes spending taxpayer money to help illegal immigrants.

> **Helping them [illegals] is the right thing to do even if it's unpopular.**
>
> —**PRICEY HARRISON,** NORTH CAROLINA STATE REPRESENTATIVE,
> **USA TODAY · JULY 7, 2008**

Josh Bernstein of the National Immigration Law Center, on the other hand, called such sweeping anti-immigration bills "a very serious threat" to the country's illegal immigrants. Bernstein is an advocate for illegal immigrants. He and other opponents of anti-immigrant education laws say education policies should not punish students for their parents' actions. North Carolina state representative Pricey Harrison, a Democrat, said, "Helping them is the right thing to do even if it's unpopular." Harrison introduced a bill that would prevent state institutions from asking about the immigration status of students.

IMMIGRANTS AND WELFARE

In the 1990s, Freddy Rios had heart surgery at Jackson Memorial Hospital in Miami, Florida. A year later, he was back in the emergency room with chest pain and fatigue. One nurse took his blood pressure. Another adjusted oxygen tubes and checked a heart monitor. A doctor recorded Freddy's medical history while a Spanish-speaking resident interpreted. The taxpayers of Miami-Dade County paid the bill, because Freddy couldn't afford it.

Freddy was an illegal immigrant from Nicaragua. In the United States, he had fathered two children by an undocumented Nicaraguan woman. Because both children are U.S. citizens, they're entitled to the same public benefits as all other citizens.

Freddy's story and others like it fuel the immigration debate. Studies and individuals on both sides of the debate reach different conclusions about whether immigrants—especially illegals—use up too much public money.

For example, most immigrants don't get welfare—because they can't. Under the 1996 welfare law (PRWORA), legal immigrants do not qualify for welfare programs for their first five years in the United States. PRWORA denies illegal immigrants all major social services funded with public money except for emergency medical care.

The Federation for American Immigration Reform (FAIR), however, challenges the idea that illegal immigrants don't get welfare. FAIR says that many immigrant families receive welfare money through their children who are U.S. citizens. And "even when immigrants are ineligible for federal welfare programs, the burden of their support is simply shifted over to the state and local welfare agencies."

Citing a Center for Immigration Studies report, FAIR said, "Each year, state governments spend an estimated eleven billion to twenty-two billion dollars to provide welfare to immigrants." The report says the highest rates of welfare use among immigrants are in New York (30

Above: A protester in Shenandoah, Pennsylvania, holds a sign stating the cost of social services for illegal immigrants. Immigration foes believe that the U.S. government shouldn't support illegal immigrants.

percent), California (28 percent), Massachusetts (25 percent), and Texas (24 percent). FAIR goes on to compare immigrant poverty and welfare use. "Immigrants are 11 percent of our population, but they are 20 percent of the poor population. Unless our immigration policies are reevaluated and changed accordingly, welfare usage and subsequent costs will remain high."

According to Congressman Ron Paul, a Texas Republican, the current U.S. welfare system is part of the problem. Knowing welfare is available, citizens are less likely to take low-paying jobs. This creates a demand for workers. Many employers turn to foreign labor to fill the jobs. And many of these foreign workers are illegal immigrants. "Welfare programs and minimum wage laws create an artificial market for labor to do the jobs Americans supposedly won't do," Paul said.

He noted, "Some illegal immigrants—certainly not all—receive housing subsidies, food stamps, free medical care, and other forms of welfare. This alienates taxpayers and breeds suspicion of immigrants, even though the majority of them work very hard. Without a welfare state, we would know that everyone coming to America wanted to work hard and support himself."

> **" Some illegal immigrants— certainly not all—receive housing subsidies, food stamps, free medical care, and other forms of welfare. This alienates taxpayers and breeds suspicion of immigrants, even though the majority of them work very hard. "**
>
> **— RON PAUL,** U.S. REPRESENTATIVE, AUGUST 2005

Paul believes that the United States should instead spend "far more of our resources, both in terms of money and manpower, to securing our borders and coastlines here at home." He added, "The problem of immigration will not be solved easily, but we can start by recognizing that the overwhelming majority of Americans—including immigrants—want immigration reduced, not expanded."

In contrast to this view, political strategist Ronald W. Wong described what he perceived to be the real issue. He wrote in *Asian Week*:

> Even if each and every one of the current anti-immigrant proposals were adopted, immigrants would continue to flock to the United States. It is an economic reality that money, goods, services, and people will flock to wealthier countries. We see this migration even within the United States as thousands have fled California for jobs in other states. Unless Mexico and other lesser developed economies grow to equal that of the United States in terms of economic opportunity, there will always be large numbers who seek a better life in America.

Wong wrote that article, titled "Eye on Politics: Fear and Loathing Fuel Anti-immigration Sentiment," in 1993. His point is still valid in the twenty-first century. Are modern immigrants really much different from those of earlier generations? The Irish, for example, fled hunger and poverty in the mid-1800s. Modern immigrants, such as those from Mexico and El Salvador, are fleeing similar problems in their home countries.

Wong concluded, "Our elected officials must be held accountable for strengthening our economy, not for outdoing each other on unworkable and unconstitutional anti-immigrant proposals. Let's work toward stopping the immigrant bashing and improving our economy, so everyone can enjoy the fruits of their labor."

IMMIGRANTS AND CRIME

Do immigrants to the United States—especially illegal aliens—raise the U.S. crime rate? Or do Americans unfairly blame them for high crime?

Peter Brimelow, an Irish immigrant and U.S. citizen, is the author of a best-selling book titled *Alien Nation*. He claims that immigrants and crime are historically linked. Brimelow, a critic of U.S. immigration policy, says crime is a "social consequence of immigration."

In his book, Brimelow quoted Ted Robert Gurr, a noted political scientist: "The United States is in the grip of the third of three great crime waves.... America's three great crime waves can be linked to *immigration*, economic deprivation and war, which all interfere with the civilizing process." [Brimelow's italics]

Tom Morganthau of *Newsweek* magazine accused Brimelow of racism. Morganthau said Brimelow thinks a successful nation must consist of citizens linked by blood. Though Brimelow never actually said other racial groups are inferior to whites, he implied it by rehashing biased statistics on welfare and the federal prison population. Morganthau concluded, "Brimelow needs reminding that the melting pot still works—and that his alarmist views of race and ethnicity are exactly what his adoptive country is trying to outgrow."

People often use statistics to bolster or deflate arguments on many issues. How reliable are statistics? They serve well as points of debate. But their meaning and importance depend on one's perspective and interpretation.

The Public Policy Institute of California (PPIC) released a study on immigrants and crime in February 2008. Its results "suggest that longstanding fears of immigration as a threat to public safety are unjustified."

The PPIC study found that people born outside the United States make up about 35 percent of California's adult population. But foreign-born people represent only about 17 percent of the state prison population. In other words, the percentage of

Above: Immigration foes fear that growing immigration means rising crime. These inmates are illegal immigrants who have committed crimes in the United States and will serve their sentences before they are deported.

immigrants in prison is much lower than the percentage of immigrants in society at large. In addition, U.S.-born adult men are jailed in state prisons at rates up to 3.3 times higher than foreign-born men. Among men ages eighteen to forty—the age group most likely to commit crime—those born in the United States are ten times more likely to be in county jail or state prison than those born outside the United States. Finally, noncitizen men from Mexico ages eighteen to forty—a group disproportionately likely to have entered the United States illegally—are more than eight times less likely than U.S.-born men in the same age group to be in a correctional setting.

Salvador Bustamante is the northern California director of Strengthening Our Lives, a statewide nonprofit group that works to empower immigrants. He applauds the PPIC study, which confirms his opinion: "A lot of people have painted immigrants as the criminal element in our society, and that isn't the case. The more we can do to dispel the myths that have been created about immigrants, [the more we] will help with immigration rights and immigration reform."

The study drew fire from immigration foes. The *Houston Chronicle* opened the story to reader comments on its website. Numerous readers responded, most of them disputing the study's findings. One reader summed up the general anti-immigration mood by saying, "I think anyone who entered or remains in my country without permission is a criminal. So, that means there are 12–20 million criminals that need to leave my country."

Crime is a real social concern in the United States. It is a pressing issue among citizens and noncitizens alike. But whether immigrants aggravate the problem remains a debated issue.

CHAPTER SIX

Culture and Morals

THE FACE OF THE UNITED STATES IS CHANGING. According to census data released in August 2008, the number of minorities in the United States is growing so rapidly that non-Hispanic whites will lose their majority status by 2042. This date falls years before demographers had projected earlier.

Change evokes strong emotions in humans. Sometimes change seems promising. Other times it seems threatening. The divergent positions Americans take on immigration often reflect these emotions.

IMMIGRANTS AND U.S. CULTURE

The idea that immigrants refuse to adopt U.S. customs and attitudes is a long-standing argument against immigration. This belief leads to fear that the United States will split into many separate cultures rather than progress as a strong and unified culture.

Writer John O'Sullivan, for example, said bluntly in the conservative magazine *National Review* that

Left: Muhamed Haidara, a Somalian refugee who came to the United States in 1991, talks with a reporter at his gift shop in Lewiston, Maine. Many U.S. cities and towns are experiencing cultural shifts and growth related to immigration.

"immigration and the multiculturalism it feeds are threatening to dissolve the bonds of common nationhood and the underlying sense of a common national destiny."

O'Sullivan argued that the arrival of more people from a variety of cultures sharpens the sense of ethnic difference among Americans. This, he said, weakens the common national identity and the sense of civic unity. According to O'Sullivan, "In periods of little or no immigration, the common national identity asserts itself; in periods of high immigration, it retreats." O'Sullivan argued that Americans are abandoning traditional values to accommodate the cultural values, morals, and practices of foreigners who live here.

David Cole of the liberal magazine the *Nation* disagrees. He notes that the claim of immigrants refusing to Americanize is not new. Americans have made this claim about every new group of immigrants to arrive on U.S. shores. For the

Above: In big U.S. cities, people from different cultures have been living side by side for decades. This barbershop in Brooklyn, New York, illustrates that reality with its window signs, which advertise the four languages its staff speak.

most part, he said, people descended from immigrants who were once considered to be separatists have created, defined, and revised U.S. culture. "Our society exerts tremendous pressure to conform," Cole argued, and cultural separatism rarely survives a generation. But more important, Cole continued, "even if this claim were true, is this a legitimate rationale for limiting immigration in a society built on the values of pluralism and tolerance?" (In a pluralist society, unique cultural groups exist side by side and consider the traits of other groups worth having in the overall society.)

In addition, Cole believes that Americans have always unfairly blamed immigrants for U.S. social problems. He labels the anti-immigration mood of the twenty-first century "the new Know-Nothingism." In an article for the *Nation*, Cole quoted a Know Nothing who wrote in 1856, "Four-fifths of the beggary [poverty] and three-fifths of the crime spring from our foreign population; more than half the

public charities, more than half the prisons and almshouses [houses for the poor], more than half the police and the cost of administering criminal justice are for foreigners." Cole believes "the Know-Nothings have returned."

Cole also points to long-standing racism in the United States as the root of anti-immigrant sentiment and unfair laws. "The objects of prejudice," he says, "are of course no longer Irish Catholics and Germans." More than 150 years later, "'they' have become 'us.' The new 'they'... are Latin Americans... Haitians and Arab-Americans, among others."

DOES RACISM PLAY A ROLE?

Immigration supporters argue that immigration foes try to instill fear and anger toward foreigners—especially Hispanics—in the general U.S. population. Immigration foes argue that their only motive is to protect U.S. society. Do racism and xenophobia (fear of foreigners) play a role in the immigration debate?

Ken Salazar, then-Democratic senator from Colorado, believes the answer is yes. He said, "I have no doubt that some . . . involved in the debate have their position based on fear and perhaps racism because of what's happening demographically in the country."

Conservative columnist Jonah Goldberg believes that labeling immigration foes "racists" is unfair. "Normal countries," Goldberg wrote, "have arguments about their national identity and immigration's effect on it. In normal countries, it's not illegitimate [wrong] to suggest that too many immigrants, or too many immigrants of a specific origin, may upset the social peace or do damage to the national culture. In America, however, to raise such concerns is to open yourself to charges of racism, bigotry [intolerance], nativism and all-around hate."

In 2006 the U.S. Senate passed a resolution declaring English the national language of the United States. This resolution was largely symbolic, since it didn't do away with bilingual education, ballots, or commerce. But according to *San Diego Union-Tribune* columnist Ruben Navarrette, even though the move was a political show, it did serve a useful purpose. "It proved once and for all, despite the insistence by many Americans that their only concern is with illegal immigration, that the truth is more complicated. We'd be more honest to admit—if there is one toxin that this country has never gotten out of its bloodstream—that it's a resentment of immigrants and foreigners regardless of their status." Navarrette noted that the immigration debate has become "an assault on the language and culture of a minority that is, in parts of the country, on its way to becoming a majority."

THE LANGUAGE DEBATE

Immigration foes argue that language is a major obstacle to Americanization. They claim that recent immigrants, especially Hispanics, refuse to learn English. This belief is common even though studies show that the vast majority of second-generation Hispanic immigrants speak English fluently.

An Ugly Debate

Ruben Navarrette, a Mexican American U.S. citizen, wrote that the current immigration debate offends him "not as a Mexican, but as an American." Navarrette is a member of the *San Diego Union-Tribune* editorial board and a nationally syndicated columnist. Here are ten things Navarrette and many other U.S.-born Hispanics find distasteful about this debate:

- The hypocrisy. We have two signs on the U.S.-Mexican border: "Keep Out" and "Help Wanted."
- The racism. With lightning speed, the debate went from anti–illegal immigrant to anti-immigrant to anti-Mexican.
- The opportunism. Too many politicians are trying too hard to portray themselves as tough on illegal immigration [to win reelection].
- The simple solutions. "Build A Wall." "Deport All Illegals." A quick rule of thumb: If it fits on a bumper sticker, it's not a workable policy.
- The naïveté. People ask why Mexico won't help stop illegal immigration. Hint: Last year, Mexicans in the United States sent home $25 billion.
- The profiling. Dark skin and Spanish surnames shouldn't be proxies [substitutes] for undocumented status. Been to Arizona lately?
- The meanness. Nazi-produced internet video games let players shoot illegal immigrants crossing the border. Fun stuff.
- The amnesia. Americans think grandpa was welcomed with open arms and that he plunged right into the melting pot. Whatever.
- The buck-passing. Americans love to blame Mexico for their choices, yelling across the border: "Stop us before we hire again."
- The double standard. The same folks who have zero tolerance for illegal immigrants easily tolerate those who hire them.

Hot rhetoric fuels Latino hate crimes

From the Pages of
USA TODAY

SEVEN TEENAGERS have been charged in the tragic death last month of Marcelo Lucero, a 38-year-old immigrant who worked at a dry cleaner. Police say Lucero was on his way to a friend's house in Patchogue, N.Y., when a gang of drunken high schoolers out to jump "a Mexican" surrounded him. Lucero was attacked and then fatally stabbed in the chest.

I suppose it doesn't matter that Patchogue is a comfortable, relatively crime-free suburb on Long Island. Or that Lucero wasn't even Mexican; he was from Ecuador. The sad truth is that Lucero's death is part of a national trend of violence against Latinos. According to new statistics from the FBI, [Hispanics] are the No. 1 target of hate crimes motivated by ethnicity or national origin. In 2007, 62% of such victims were Hispanic.

Yet these statistics might not show the full picture. A 2005 Justice Department report asserted that the actual number of hate crimes exceeded the FBI's numbers. The Southern Poverty Law Center, a civil rights group, confirms that many hate crimes are not reported. Many

The drive for a law to make English the official U.S. language is picking up steam. Supporters are filling ballots with measures that discourage bilingual notices, ballots, and other official documents.

According to a *USA TODAY* article, as of June 2008, thirty states had laws requiring English for official government communications. A group called U.S. English, based in Washington, D.C., promotes English-only laws. Its chairman, Mauro Mujica, says an additional nineteen state legislatures are considering such laws. "[The movement is] multiplying tremendously; we've made huge illegal immigrants, no doubt fearing deportation, would be reluctant to contact law enforcement.

The Patchogue killing reminds me of an incident this summer in Shenandoah, Pa., in which four teens were charged in the death of an illegal Mexican immigrant.

What do these two communities have in common? An increase in the Latino population and a corresponding rise in anti-immigrant sentiments.

Today, the national anti-immigration fervor has subsided as the economy has cooled, but it's fair to assume that some violence against Latinos is a byproduct of the xenophobic debate of previous years. Hate crimes directed at Latinos rose 40% during the past four years—a time frame that roughly corresponds to the failure of attempts at comprehensive reform. Some politicians and activists who oppose illegal immigration often have engaged in or encouraged anti-Hispanic rhetoric. They don't seem to realize that inflammatory language can incite inflammatory acts.

It saddens and angers me that Latinos must still live with the threat of violence simply because of their ethnicity. I am worried, too, that in these tough economic times, fear and anxiety will be directed at the wrong targets. Hate speech can hurt, and sometimes kill.

If and when this country revisits the immigration issue under an Obama administration, we should engage in a debate that is good for all of us—rather than one that vilifies and endangers some of us.

—Raul Reyes, from the Opinion page

progress," says Mujica, an immigrant from Chile.

Critics of English-only laws don't see the new laws as progress. In fact, many say the increase of such laws sends a hostile message to newcomers. "It just poisons the atmosphere in local communities," said John Trasviña, president of the Mexican American Legal Defense and Educational Fund (MALDEF).

Typically, English-only laws require printing government documents, ballots, and other official communications only in English. The laws usually allow communications that protect public health and safety or encourage tourism, such as signs, to remain multilingual.

Mujica and other advocates of English-only laws say they don't want English to be the only language spoken in the United States. But they do want English to be the only language used in government dealings. Mujica speaks Spanish in his home. He says requiring English for official business encourages immigrants to learn the language. By learning English, immigrants will Americanize and prosper in the United States more quickly. "We're making it too easy for people to function in other languages," Mujica said.

English-only state laws may run into roadblocks because of federal laws, however. The federal Voting Rights Act of 1965 requires certain communities to publish bilingual ballots. According to the act, any city that receives a request for bilingual ballots must provide them.

Trasviña said the U.S. English campaign has only served to raise "the level of ire [anger] against languages other than English." But it hasn't actually changed the way government and business function.

Rob Toonkel, a spokesman for U.S. English, says Trasviña's claim is false. According to Toonkel, the English-only laws are not meant to cover all communication. They do ensure that day-to-day public activities and government

Above: In 2002 Minnesota secretary of state Mary Kiffmeyer revealed a multilingual voter instruction poster. The poster includes instructions in Hmong, Spanish, Somali, and Russian.

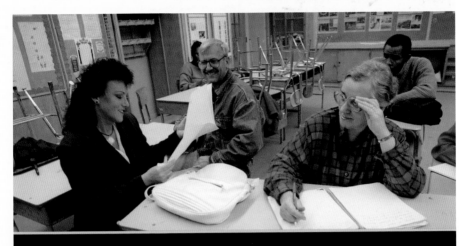

Above: Eva Spinelli teaches English as a second language (ESL) classes at Mercy College in Brooklyn, New York. Immigration foes and supporters agree that the United States could do more to help immigrants learn English.

documents such as driver's licenses and zoning forms are overwhelmingly in English. "We want to be sure [immigrants] are becoming part of America and American society," Toonkel said. "That's what official English is all about."

The two sides do agree on one issue. Both believe that the United States could do more to help immigrants learn English. Sam Jammal, an attorney in MALDEF's Washington, D.C., office, said making English classes more available for adult immigrants is a better solution to language issues than the official English movement. "We fully agree with that," said Mujica.

MORAL RESPONSIBILITY

Does the United States have a moral responsibility to admit a certain number of legal immigrants? And does the nation have a moral responsibility to provide basic services to newcomers, even if some of them are illegal immigrants? Arguments over that question have echoed in homes, coffee shops, town halls, and lawmakers' chambers for many decades.

In his book *Alien Nation*, Peter Brimelow addressed the issue of morality by posing the following question:

> **If immigration is . . . a moral imperative, why don't the Mexicans/Chinese/Indians/Koreans/Japanese . . . allow it?** [Brimelow's bold type] Don't say: "These countries already have enough people." The United States already has more than all of them except mainland China and India. And don't say: "They're too poor." As we have seen, the whole economic theory of immigration, as developed by immigration enthusiasts, is that immigration does not displace workers: it complements them.

Brimelow reported calling the Chinese Embassy in Washington to ask about immigration. An official laughed and said, "China does not accept any immigrants. We have a large enough population." Brimelow then cited negative responses from other embassies asked the same question. He noted that China, Mexico, South Korea, and India send thousands of immigrants to the United States every year.

Brimelow said, "*The world is laughing at America.*" He suggested that "the critics of immigration adopt a name that has a long and honorable role in

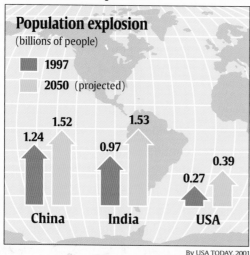

USA TODAY Snapshots®

Population explosion
(billions of people)

■ 1997
▢ 2050 (projected)

China 1.24 → 1.52
India 0.97 → 1.53
USA 0.27 → 0.39

By USA TODAY, 2001

Above: Illegal Vietnamese immigrants to Hong Kong, China, await deportation. Anti-immigration Americans say the United States should follow other countries' examples of intolerance for illegal entries.

American history. They should call themselves—'*Patriots.*'" [Brimelow's italics]

Despite statements like Brimelow's, U.S. church leaders generally abhor anti-immigration movements. Debate over the McCain-Kennedy immigration bill prompted many religious leaders to speak out.

In 2006 the presiding bishop of the Episcopal Church, Katharine Jefferts Schori, said, "I continue to be reminded that Jesus and his family were refugees in Egypt. Will we recognize him when he wanders into our midst? Will we invite the stranger to join us, in full and exuberant welcome? Will we work together to build a home for all God's children?" Jefferts Schori, the bishops, and the Executive Council of the Episcopal Church issued a statement calling for immigration reform that "results in U.S. policy that is in sync with the gospel mandate to welcome the stranger among us."

USA TODAY Snapshots®

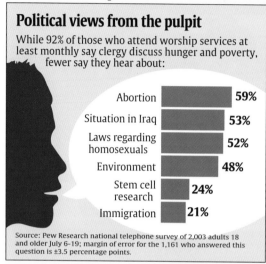

Political views from the pulpit

While 92% of those who attend worship services at least monthly say clergy discuss hunger and poverty, fewer say they hear about:

Abortion	59%
Situation in Iraq	53%
Laws regarding homosexuals	52%
Environment	48%
Stem cell research	24%
Immigration	21%

Source: Pew Research national telephone survey of 2,003 adults 18 and older July 6-19; margin of error for the 1,161 who answered this question is ±3.5 percentage points.

By Tracey Wong Briggs and Veronica Salazar, USA TODAY, 2006

Meanwhile, Methodist Church leaders called upon Congress to "adopt comprehensive immigration policy that respects the full human rights of all immigrants." R. Randy Day, chief executive of the United Methodist Board of Global Ministries, said, "This should include full labor protections, family reunification, preservation of due process and a path to genuine legalization."

The McCain-Kennedy bill collapsed in 2007 largely because it included a path to citizenship for illegals. Conservative politicians and their constituents considered this provision the same as amnesty (pardon).

Former Department of Homeland Security secretary Michael Chertoff said he knows most illegal immigrants come here to work and many are fleeing difficult circumstances. "But I can't condone their violation of the law," he said. "However heart-wrenching the motive is, it is still a violation of the law to sneak in."

> **"However heart-wrenching the motive is, it is still a violation of the law to sneak in [to the United States].**"
>
> **—MICHAEL CHERTOFF,**
> FORMER DHS SECRETARY, 2008

In January 2008, the international Catholic Church became directly involved in illegal immigration. The Vatican (headquarters of the Roman Catholic Church) donated thousands of dollars to help the Brothers on the Path charity build an immigrant shelter in Ixtepec, a city in southern Mexico. According to a *USA TODAY* report, "The area around Ixtepec is a major conduit [pathway] of Central American migrants who ride freight trains to the U.S. border." Alejandro Solalinde, a priest and director of the shelter project, said that many Catholic churches in the United States and Mexico have programs to help immigrants. But "few receive direct support from the Vatican."

The money angered U.S. immigration foes. Al Garza, executive director of the Minuteman Civil Defense

Above: These illegal immigrants from Guatemala are bound for the United States. They rest at a shelter in Ixtepec, Mexico. The shelter received a large donation from the Vatican, headquarters of the Catholic Church in Rome.

Corps, a volunteer border-watch group, called the shelter "sinful." He added, "What they're really doing is saying, 'Look, even though the United States has laws, we're going to help you break the laws to realize your dream.'"

Jack Martin of the Federation for American Immigration Reform said that by funding the shelter, the Vatican was "undertaking policies that had the effect of facilitating illegal immigration to this country." Further, he said, the Vatican had an interest in immigration "that derives from the fact that the majority of illegal immigration into the [United States] is from Catholic countries. It helps fill the pews, it helps fill the coffers [bank accounts], it helps fill the recruits to the priesthood."

Catholic officials defended the gift as a humanitarian gesture. Kevin Appleby, director of migration and refugee policy for the National Conference of Catholic Bishops, said, "The

Above: Members of the Minuteman Civil Defense Corps, a volunteer border-watch organization, help construct a barbed-wire fence on private land along the U.S.–Mexico border in Palominas, Arizona.

church's mission is to provide assistance to people in need. We're not a law enforcement group."

PRO-IMMIGRATION PATRIOTS

Immigration advocates, like immigration foes, see themselves as patriots. In his 1963 book *A Nation of Immigrants*, President John F. Kennedy drew a parallel between immigrant-bashing and the birth of this country. Kennedy wrote:

> Immigration, or rather the British policy of clamping down on immigration, was one of the factors behind the Colonial desire for independence. Restrictive immigration policies constituted one of the charges against King George III [of England] expressed in the Declaration of Independence. And in the Constitutional Convention, James Madison noted, "That part of America which has encouraged them [the immigrants] has advanced most rapidly in population, agriculture and the arts."

Above: Members of a U.S. labor union rally in support of immigrants' rights in New York City.

Colin Powell, a former U.S. secretary of state and widely respected retired four-star general, addressed the issue of immigration at the Republican Party's national convention in 1996. He told the assembly:

> A nation as great and diverse as America deserves leadership that opens its arms not only to those who have already reaped the rewards of the American dream, but to those who strive and struggle each day often against daunting odds to make that dream come true.

Above: Two young people attend a rally in Shenandoah, Pennsylvania, to protest immigration.

> The Hispanic immigrant who became a citizen yesterday must be as precious to us as a *Mayflower* descendant—the descendant of a slave or of a struggling miner in Appalachia [a mountainous region of the eastern United States] must be as welcome in our party as any other American.

Powell addressed the Republican convention again in 2000, saying in part, "Immigration is part of our life's blood. It's part of the essence of who we are as Americans. I am the son of immigrants." Powell went on to become the U.S. secretary of state during the first

> **If and when this country revisits the immigration issue . . . we should engage in a debate that is good for all of us. . . .**
>
> **—RAUL REYES,** USA TODAY COLUMNIST
> **USA TODAY · DECEMBER 5, 2008**

term of President George W. Bush (2001–2005).

The opposing immigration forces are equally American and equally patriotic. But they remain divided.

THE NEXT CHAPTER

The United States, formed and fueled by immigrants, has swelled to a population of more than three hundred million people. Some say, "This is all we can handle—shut the door." Others point to the nation's golden door and say, "This is our heritage—come, join us."

The United States has accepted more immigrants than any other country on Earth. How can Americans explain this?

Do Americans, as descendants of immigrants, have a moral or civic duty to open the nation's door to immigrants?

If so, how can this be done in a safer, more orderly, and more productive way?

Do people in other lands see opportunities in the United States that their countries don't offer? If so, should Americans use more resources for the economic, political, and social development of other countries, as a way to curb immigration to the United States?

What will be the consequences if the United States continues to open the door? Or if the nation slams the door shut? The youth of the early twenty-first century will write the answers to all these questions. And then a new chapter will begin.

As Bernard Weisberger wrote in *American Heritage,* "So it is that immigration regularly returns to the news. It always has. It always does."

TIMELINE

30,000–12,000 B.C.	Nomads follow the Bering land bridge from Siberia to North America searching for food and fur.
A.D. 1492	Christopher Columbus arrives in the Americas.
1513	The Spanish build a colony near Saint Augustine, Florida.
1608	French fur traders establish the city of Quebec in Canada.
1620	The *Mayflower* lands at Plymouth, Massachusetts.
1682	French explorers travel down the Mississippi River, setting up trading posts at Saint Louis (Missouri) and New Orleans (Louisiana).
1775	The Revolutionary War begins.
1776	The United States of America declares independence from Great Britain.
1783	The Revolutionary War ends.
1790	A federal naturalization law restricts citizenship to white Americans.
1803	The United States buys 828,000 square miles (2.1 million sq. km) of new land west of the Mississippi River in a deal known as the Louisiana Purchase.
1820–1890	About five million European immigrants arrive in the United States, mostly from Ireland and Germany.
1839–1842	The First Opium War takes place in China.
1845–1847	The Irish potato famine leaves millions of Irish people starving, spurring immigration to the United States.
1855	The nativist political movement develops into a national party, the American Party, and becomes known as the Know Nothings.

1856–1860	The Second Opium War occurs in China.
1861–1865	The American Civil War pits the North against the South.
1882	The Chinese Exclusion Act bans Chinese immigrants from entering the United States.
1886	France presents the Statue of Liberty to the United States.
1892	Ellis Island opens in New York, becoming the U.S. government's official immigrant processing center.
1894	The Boston-based Immigration Restriction League forms.
1914–1918	World War I is fought on battlefields across Europe and in Turkey.
1924	The Johnson-Reed Act sets strict immigrant quotas. Congress forms the U.S. Border Patrol.
1929	The National Origins Act refines immigrant quotas set by the Johnson-Reed Act.
1939–1945	World War II is fought on battlefields around the globe. The United States joins the war in 1941.
1945	The War Brides Act admits foreign spouses and children of U.S. World War II soldiers into the United States.
1948, 1950	Two versions of the Displaced Persons Act let European refugees settle in the United States.
1952	The McCarran-Walter Act combines all immigration laws into one and limits immigration from Eastern Europe.
1965	The Hart-Celler Act ends immigration quotas based on nationality and establishes "preference quotas."
1996	Congress enacts the Illegal Immigration Reform and Immigrant Responsibility Act (IIRIRA) and the Personal Responsibility and Work Opportunity Reconciliation Act (PRWORA).

2001 Terrorist attacks kill thousands in New York City; near Washington, D.C.; and in rural Pennsylvania. Many illegal immigrants flee New York City in the wake of the attacks.

2006 About twelve million illegal immigrants live in the United States. Hazleton, Pennsylvania, enacts a harsh city immigration law. ICE agents raid meatpacking plants in six states, arresting 1,297 people. Senators John McCain and Ted Kennedy cosponsor a bill that would enable illegal immigrants to gain citizenship.

2007 The McCain-Kennedy bill dies in the Senate. Oklahoma enacts the Oklahoma Taxpayer and Citizen Protection Act to drive illegal immigrants out of Oklahoma.

2008 ICE agents raid workplaces in Postville, Iowa, and Laurel, Mississippi, arresting hundreds of illegal workers. Republican senators introduce fourteen anti-immigration bills in a single day. The U.S. Census Bureau projects the U.S. population will grow from three hundred million to four hundred million in thirty-one years. The United States completes 553 miles (890 km) of fence along the Mexican border.

2009 Some U.S. states, counties, and cities repeal or modify their harsh immigration laws. The House Committee on Homeland Security conducts hearings to examine a federal program that deputizes local police officers to act as immigration enforcement agents. The DHS announced a plan to add hundreds more agents to the U.S.–Mexico border, to begin monitoring outbound traffic for illegal weapons and cash, and to refocus workplace raids on employers who knowingly hire illegal immigrants. Jiverly Wong kills thirteen people and himself at an immigrant aid center in Binghamton, New York. President Obama appoints a "border czar" to handle illegal immigration and drug violence problems along the U.S.–Mexico border.

GLOSSARY

alien: a foreigner; in legal terms, a resident of one country born in or belonging to another country. An alien has not acquired citizenship by naturalization.

amnesty: pardon

assimilate: to adapt to the culture of a particular society; to absorb newcomers into a society

asylum: protection from arrest and removal given by one country to a refugee from another country

bipartisan: cooperative, two-party

conservatives: people who support established institutions and cultural norms and who generally favor a limited role for government. In political spheres, conservatives are often called the Right.

constituents: the voters or residents of an area represented by an elected official

demographics: the statistical traits of a population, such as nationality and economic status

deport: to expel; to send out of the country

emigration: leaving one country to live in another. The prefix *e-* means "out of," and the prefix *im-* means "into." Someone who moves from one country to another emigrates from the former and immigrates to the latter.

immigrant: a person who moves to make a home in a new country

liberals: people who support the idea that institutions and cultural norms can change as societal attitudes shift and who generally support a broad role for government. In political spheres, liberals are often called the Left.

multiculturalism: the preservation of different cultures within a unified society

nativist: favoring the interests of native-born residents over those of immigrants

refugee: a person who escapes danger or persecution in his or her home country by fleeing to another country

sanctuary: a place of refuge or protection

sojourner: a temporary immigrant who intends to make money and eventually return home

sponsor: someone who agrees to support or employ an immigrant for a specific period of time. A sponsor is a U.S. citizen or lawful permanent resident who is an immediate relative of an immigrant. A sponsor may also be a U.S. employer or an adoptive parent who is a U.S. citizen.

subsidies: government funds made available to help people, institutions, or organizations. A government subsidizes efforts it considers good for the general public, such as education, medical care, housing, and so on.

undocumented: lacking documents required for legal immigration or residence

visa: a government document allowing an individual to remain in the country ruled by that government for a certain length of time

SOURCE NOTES

7 Bernard A. Weisberger, "A Nation of Immigrants," *American Heritage*, February–March 1994, 80.

9 Joint Committee on Printing, "The Constitution of the United States with Index and the Declaration of Independence," *U.S. Government Printing Office*, July 5, 2007, http://frwebgate.access.gpo.gov/cgi-bin/getdoc.cgi?dbname=110 _cong_documents&docid=f:hd051.110.pdf (January 12, 2009).

9 Edward Kennedy, "Statement of Senator Edward M. Kennedy on Comprehensive Immigration Reform," *Senator Edward M. Kennedy: United States Senator for Massachusetts*, May 21, 2007, http://kennedy.senate.gov/ issues_and_agenda/issue.cfm?id=df725284-80e8-4f31-91c5 -ede8f37047c2 (January 21, 2009).

10 Michael Mandel, "Bordering on Absurdity," *BusinessWeek*, May 26, 2006, http://www.businessweek.com/investor/content/may2006/ pi20060526_553811.htm (January 20, 2009).

10 *Time* editors, "America's Immigrant Challenge," *Time* special issue, Fall 1993, 9.

10 Emma Lazarus, "The New Colossus," *Statue of Liberty National Monument: History and Culture*, October 5, 2006, http://www.nps.gov/stli/ historyculture/index.htm (January 11, 2009).

11 Ibid.

18 Weisberger, 80.

18 Ibid.

20 Brent Ashabranner, *Still a Nation of Immigrants* (New York: Cobblehill Books, 1993), 15.

21 John Elson, "The Great Migration," *Time* special issue, Fall 1993, 31–32.

22 Ibid., 32.

26 Ibid.

29 Theodore Roosevelt, "Theodore Roosevelt (December 3, 1906)," *Collected State of the Union Addresses of U.S. Presidents*, n.d., http:www.infoplease .com/t/hist/state-of-the-union/118.html (January 11, 2009).

31–32 Gerald Leinwand, *American Immigration: Should the Open Door Be Closed?* (New York: Franklin Watts, 1995), 52.

33 James S. Pula, *Polish Americans: An Ethnic Community* (New York: Twayne Publishers, 1995), 64.

33 Ibid.

33 Leinwand, 64.

33   Weisberger, 86.

37   Lyndon B. Johnson, "President Lyndon B. Johnson's Remarks at the Signing of the Immigration Bill, Liberty Island, New York: October 3, 1965," *Lyndon Baines Johnson Library and Museum*, June 6, 2007, http://www.lbjlib.utexas .edu/johnson/archives.hom/speeches.hom/651003.asp (January 12, 2009).

39   Weisberger, 89.

39   William Dunn, "Sun Belt Gets More People, More Clout," *USA TODAY*, December 29, 1989.

43   Mary Jacoby, "Immigration Bill Targets Legals, Too," *Chicago Tribune*, August 27, 1996.

43   Ibid.

43   Ibid.

43   Carol Jouzaitis, "Cuts in U.S. Food Aid Likely to Tighten Belt for Millions," *Chicago Tribune*, August 18, 1996.

44   Ibid.

47   *USA TODAY* editors, "Latest Immigration 'Crisis' Defies Simplistic Solutions," *USA TODAY*, March 30, 2006.

50   Kathy Kiely, "Public Favors Giving Illegal Immigrants in the USA a Break," *USA TODAY*, April 19, 2007.

51   Ibid.

51   Ibid.

51   *Washington Times*, "McCain '08 Bid Losing Steam," June 13, 2007, http:// www.washingtontimes.com/news/2007/jun/13/20070613-120640-7717r/ (January 12, 2009).

51   Kiely, "Public Favors Giving Illegal Immigrants in the USA a Break."

51, 54   *USA TODAY* editors, "Washington's Failure Triggers Anti-immigrant Backlash," *USA TODAY*, August 15, 2007.

54   Kathy Kiely, "Immigration Overhaul Crumbles in Senate Vote," *USA TODAY*, June 29, 2007.

61   Bill Hughes, "Opinion: The Immigration Conundrum," *Oakland Post*, July 20, 1994.

64   Michael Powell and Michelle García, "Pa. City Puts Illegal Immigrants on Notice," *Washingtonpost.com*, August 22, 2006, http://www.washingtonpost.com/wp -dyn/content/article/2006/08/21/AR2006082101484.html (January 12, 2009).

64   Ibid.

65   *USA TODAY* editors, "Washington's Failure Triggers Anti-immigrant Backlash."

65 Marisa Treviño, "Senate Inaction Means More Hate Directed at Innocent Legal Immigrants," *Latina Lista*, June 8, 2007, http://www.latinalista.net/ palabrafinal/2007/06/senate_inaction_means_more_hate_directed.html (January 25, 2009).

65 Tracie Mauriello, "Rally Backs Hazleton Mayor," *Pittsburgh Post-Gazette*, June 4, 2007.

66 Kathy Kiely, "Touchy Issue of Immigration Is Pols' Touchstone," *USA TODAY*, April 25, 2008.

66 Joel Dyer, "Meatpacking Industry Has a Long History of Reliance on Immigrant Laborer," *GreeleyTribune.com*, December 26, 2006, http://www .greeleytribune.com/article/20061226/NEWS/112230087 (January 25, 2009).

68 Judy Keen, "Tensions Grip Minnesota City," *USA TODAY*, August 29, 2008.

68 Ibid.

69 Ibid.

69 Ibid.

69 Ibid.

69–70 Ibid.

70 Raul Reyes, "Time to Dispel Those Immigrant Myths," *USA TODAY*, December 28, 2007.

70 Ibid.

70 Ibid.

71 Keen.

71 Ibid.

74 Emily Bazar, "Lawmakers Seek 'Sanctuary Cities' Crackdown," *USA TODAY*, October 25, 2007.

75 Ibid.

81 *USA TODAY* editors, "Latest Immigration 'Crisis' Defies Simplistic Solutions."

83 Paulette Chu Miniter, "A Border Agent (and Immigrant) Defies Stereotypes," *USA TODAY*, May 8, 2007.

83 Miniter.

84 Ibid.

84 Mimi Hall, "Homeland Security Dept. Waives Laws to Finish Fence on U.S.-Mexican Border," *USA TODAY*, April 2, 2008.

84 Ibid.

84–85 Ibid.

86 Marisa Treviño, "Texans Raising Voices against Border Fence," *USA TODAY*, August 10, 2007.

87 Elliot Spagat, "Construction Underway of $57M San Diego Border Fence," *USA TODAY*, August 15, 2008.

87 Ibid.

87 Ibid.

88 Thomas Frank, "Tensions Up with Border Fence," *USA TODAY*, December 29, 2008.

88 Luis Alberto Urrea, "$1.2 Billion Fence Adds Little or No Security," *San Francisco Chronicle*, February 10, 2008.

88 Ibid.

88 Ibid.

88 Frank.

89 Ibid.

89 Hearst Communications, "Comments: $1.2 Billion Fence Adds Little or No Security," *SFGate.com*, February 11, 2008, http://www.sfgate.com/cgi-bin/ article/comments/view?f=/c/a/2008/02/10/IN25UJSCR.DTL (January 28, 2009).

89 Frank.

91 Jackson.

91 Ibid.

91 Musaffar Chishti and Claire Bergeron, "Iowa Raid Raises Questions about Stepped-Up Immigration Enforcement," *Migration Information Source*, June 16, 2008, http://www.migrationinformation.org/USfocus/display .cfm?id=686 (January 12, 2009).

91 Holbrook Mohr, "Fear Grips Immigrants after Raid at Mississippi Plant," *USA TODAY*, August 27, 2008.

92 Henry C. Jackson, "Town Wonders If It's Next to Face Immigration Raid," *USA TODAY*, August 26, 2008.

96 Raul Reyes, "What Are ICE Raids Accomplishing?" *USA TODAY*, August 8, 2008.

96 Ginger Thompson, "Immigration Agents to Turn Focus to Employers," *New York Times*, April 30, 2009.

96 Reyes, "What Are ICE Raids Accomplishing?"

97 Emily Bazar, "Strict Immigration Law Rattles Okla. Businesses," *USA TODAY*, January 10, 2008.

98 Bazar, "Strict Immigration Law Rattles Okla. Businesses."

98 Ibid.

98 Ibid.

99 Ibid.

99 Ibid.

100 Ibid.

100 Ibid.

101 Emily Bazar, "Illegal Immigrants Moving Out," *USA TODAY*, September 27, 2007.

101 Ibid.

101 Ibid.

101 Ibid.

103 Paul Overberg and Emily Bazar, "America's Face Evolves, Blurs, Ages," *USA TODAY*, August 14, 2008.

104 Immigrant Learning Center, "Immigrants, Jobs, and the Labor Force," *The ILC in the News*, n.d., http://www.ilctr.org/news/pdf/imm_job_and_labor.pdf (January 12, 2009).

104 Ibid.

105 Nick Miroff, "Immigrants' Jobs Vanish with Housing Slowdown," *Washingtonpost.com*, December 27, 2006, http://www.washingtonpost.com/wp-dyn/content/article/2006/12/26/AR2006122601121.html (January 12, 2009).

108 Ibid.

108 Mary Beth Marklein, "Illegal Immigrants Face Threat of No College," *USA TODAY*, July 7, 2008.

109 Ibid.

109 Ibid.

109 Ibid.

110 Federation for American Immigration Reform, "Immigration and Welfare," *Immigration Issues: Labor and Economics*, October 2002, http://www.fairus.org/site/PageServer?pagename=iic_immigrationissuecenters7fd8 (January 12, 2009).

110 Ibid.

111 Ibid.

111 Ron Paul, "Immigration and the Welfare State," *LewRockwell.com*, August 9, 2005, http://www.lewrockwell.com/paul/paul269.html (January 12, 2009).

111 Ibid.

111 Ibid.

112 Ibid.

112 Ronald W. Wong, "Eye on Politics: Fear and Loathing Fuel Anti-immigration Sentiment," *Asian Week*, October 22, 1993, 11.

109 Ibid.

113 Peter Brimelow, *Alien Nation* (New York: Random House, 1995), 182.

113 Ibid.

113 Tom Morganthau, "Fear of an Immigrant Nation," *Newsweek*, May 8, 1995, 63.

113 Kristin F. Butcher and Anne Morrison Piehl, "Immigration Has Little to Do with California Crime," *Public Policy Institute of California*, February 25, 2008, http://www.ppic.org/main/pressrelease.asp?i=812 (January 12, 2009).

114–115 Javier Erik Olvera, "Migrants Unlikely to End Up in Prison," *MercuryNews.com*, February 26, 2008, http://www.mercurynews.com/ci_8365551 (January 12, 2009).

115 *Houston Chronicle* staff, "Immigration Chronicles: Immigrants, Crime and California," *Chron.com*, April 19, 2008, http://blogs.chron.com/immigration/archives/2008/04/post_117.html (January 12, 2009).

118 John O'Sullivan, "America's Identity Crisis," *National Review*, November 21, 1994, 44.

118 Ibid.

119 David Cole, "Five Myths about Immigration," *Nation*, October 17, 1994, 412.

119 Ibid., 410.

119 Ibid.

120 Massimo Calabresi, "Is Racism Fueling the Immigration Debate?" *Time.com*, May 17, 2006, http://www.time.com/time/nation/article/0,8599,1195250,00.html (February 2, 2009).

120 Jonah Goldberg, "You Can't Say That," *USA TODAY*, July 3, 2007.

120 Ruben Navarrette Jr., "Racism Surfaces in Immigration Debate," *SignOnSanDiego.com*, May 24, 2006, http://www.signonsandiego.com/uniontrib/20060524/news_lz1e24navarre.html (February 2, 2009).

121 Ruben Navarrette Jr., "Commentary: 10 Ugly Things about the Immigration Debate," *CNNPolitics.com*, April 28, 2008, http://www.cnn.com/2008/POLITICS/04/28/navarrette/index.html (January 13, 2009).

121 Ibid.

122–123 William M. Welch, "English-Only Laws Gathering Steam," *USA TODAY*, June 19, 2008.

123 Ibid.

124 Ibid.

125 Ibid.

126 Brimelow, 250–251.

126–127 Ibid., 254.

127 Katharine Jefferts Schori, "Welcome the Stranger, and Care for the Alien in Your Midst," *Episcopal Migration Ministries*, 2006, http://www .episcopalchurch.org/3687_99378_ENG_HTM.htm?menu=undefined (January 12, 2009).

127 Episcopal Church USA, "Immigration Reform," *Episcopal Migration Ministries*, 2006, http://www.ecusa.anglican.org/3687_74625_ENG_HTM .htm?menu=menu32080 (January 12, 2009).

128 Kathy Gilbert, "Immigration Bill Falls Short, United Methodist Leaders Say," *Worldwide Faith News Archives*, May 26, 2006, http://www.wfn .org/2006/05/msg00234.html (January 12, 2009).

128 Emily Bazar, "After Deportation, Migrants Are Determined to Return," *USA TODAY*, March 24, 2008.

129 Ibid.

129 Chris Hawley and Sergio Solache, "Vatican Aid to Immigrants Raises Ire in USA," *USA TODAY*, April 16, 2008.

129 Ibid.

130 Ibid.

130 Ibid.

130–131 Ibid.

131 John F. Kennedy, *A Nation of Immigrants* (New York: Harper & Row, 1964), 69.

132 Colin Powell, "Value Today's Immigrant as Much as Mayflower Descendant," *On the Issues: Colin Powell on Immigration*, August 12, 1996, http://www.ontheissues.org/Celeb/Colin_Powell_Immigration.htm (January 13, 2009).

132 Colin Powell, "Immigration Is Part of Our Life's Blood," *On the Issues: Colin Powell on Immigration*, July 30, 2000, http://www.ontheissues.org/Celeb/ Colin_Powell_Immigration.htm (January 13, 2009).

133 Raul Reyes, "Hot Rhetoric Fuels Latino Hate Crimes," *USA TODAY*, December 5, 2008.

133 Weisberger, 76.

SELECTED BIBLIOGRAPHY

Ashabranner, Brent. *Still a Nation of Immigrants*. New York: Cobblehill Books, 1993.

Bazar, Emily. "Lawmakers Seek 'Sanctuary Cities' Crackdown." *USA TODAY*, October 25, 2007.

——. "Strict Immigration Law Rattles Okla. Businesses." *USA TODAY*, January 10, 2008.

Brimelow, Peter. *Alien Nation*. New York: Random House, 1995.

Butcher, Kristin F., and Anne Morrison Piehl. "Immigraton Has Little to Do with California Crime." *Public Policy Institute of California*. February 25, 2008. http://www.ppic.org/main/pressrelease.asp?i=812 (January 12, 2009).

Cox, Vic. *The Challenge of Immigration*. Springfield, NJ: Enslow, 1995.

Hardin, Garrett. *The Immigration Dilemma: Avoiding the Tragedy of the Commons*. Washington, DC: Federation for American Immigration Reform, 1995.

"Immigration Polls." *Immigrationpolls.com*. 2007. http://www .immigrationpolls.com (January 13, 2009).

Kennedy, John F. *A Nation of Immigrants*. New York: Harper & Row, 1964.

Kiely, Kathy. "Public Favors Giving Illegal Immigrants in the USA a Break." *USA TODAY*, April 19, 2007.

——. "Touchy Issue of Immigration Is Pols' Touchstone." *USA TODAY*, April 25, 2008.

Leinwand, Gerald. *American Immigration: Should the Open Door Be Closed?* New York: Franklin Watts, 1995.

Navarrette, Ruben, Jr. "Commentary: 10 Ugly Things about the Immigration Debate." *CNNPolitics.com*. April 28, 2008. http://www.cnn .com/2008/POLITICS/04/28/navarrette/index.html (January 13, 2009).

Overberg, Paul, and Emily Bazar. "America's Face Evolves, Blurs, Ages." *USA TODAY*, August 14, 2008.

Time editors. "America's Immigrant Challenge." *Time* special issue, Fall 1993.

USA TODAY editors. "Latest Immigration 'Crisis' Defies Simplistic Solutions." *USA TODAY*, March 30, 2006.

——. "No More Hollow Solutions." *USA TODAY*, November 16, 2006.

——. "Washington's Failure Triggers Anti-immigrant Backlash." *USA TODAY*, August 15, 2007.

Weisberger, Bernard A. "A Nation of Immigrants." *American Heritage*, February–March 1994.

Wolf, Richard. "Rising Health Care Costs Put Focus on Migrants." *USA TODAY*, January 22, 2008.

ORGANIZATIONS TO CONTACT

American Immigration Control Foundation (AICF)
P.O. Box 525
Monterey, VA 24465
540-468-2022
http://www.aicfoundation.com
AICF is a nonprofit research and educational organization. Its main goal is to inform Americans of the need for a reasonable immigration policy based on U.S. interests and the nation's capacity to assimilate newcomers. AICF publishes and distributes publications on the U.S. immigration crisis. The organization is particularly concerned about illegal immigration over the Mexican border. AICF argues that such immigration adds a large burden to already excessive legal quotas, weakens our rule of law, and puts the future of our country in jeopardy.

Americans for Immigration Control (AIC)
P.O. Box 738
Monterey, VA 24465
540-468-2023
http://www.immigrationcontrol.com
AIC is a nonpartisan grassroots activist organization founded in 1983. AIC seeks to stop illegal immigrants who come into the United States and supports deporting those illegals already in the country. AIC opposes amnesty and guest worker programs and advocates increasing penalties for those who knowingly transport, recruit, solicit, or hire illegal immigrants.

Center for Immigrants' Rights (CIR)
48 Saint Mark's Place, 4th Floor
New York, NY 10003
212-505-6890
http://www.dvguide.com/newyork/cir.html
For more than twenty years, CIR has engaged in important litigation, including numerous class action cases, on behalf of immigrants and refugees. CIR also funds organizations around the country to provide representation to vulnerable immigrants. CIR has won major court victories and nationwide settlements requiring that

• all arrested immigrants must be informed of their right to counsel;

• all immigrants appearing before immigration judges must be advised of local free legal services available;

• all detained immigrant minors are eligible for release to licensed shelters and responsible third parties other than their parents;

• all undocumented children may attend public school.

Federation for American Immigration Reform (FAIR)
25 Massachusetts Avenue NW, Suite 300
Washington, DC 20001
202-328-7004
http://www.fairus.org
FAIR is a national, nonprofit, membership organization. Members share a belief in reforming U.S. immigration policies to serve U.S. interests. FAIR seeks to improve border security, to stop illegal immigration, and to promote immigration levels consistent with the national interest (about three hundred thousand immigrants per year). FAIR is a nonpartisan group. Congress has called FAIR to testify on immigration bills more often than any other U.S. organization.

National Immigration Forum (NIF)
50 F Street NW, Suite 300
Washington, DC 20001
202-347-0040
http://www.immigrationforum.org
NIF formed in 1982 and is the nation's foremost immigrant rights organization. It is dedicated to embracing and upholding the United States' heritage as a nation of immigrants. NIF advocates and builds

public support for policies that welcome immigrants and refugees and that are fair to and supportive of newcomers. NIF does not have a specific constituency but speaks for immigration in the national interest. NIF has been the driving force behind many immigration policy victories and works closely with local advocates and service providers across the country.

National Immigration Law Center (NILC)
3435 Wilshire Boulevard, Suite 2850
Los Angeles, CA 90010
213-639-3900
http://www.nilc.org
Founded in 1979, NILC is dedicated to protecting and promoting the rights of low-income immigrants and their families. In the past twenty years, NILC has earned a national reputation as a leading expert on immigration, public benefits, and employment laws affecting immigrants and refugees. NILC's extensive knowledge of the complex interplay between immigrants' legal status and their rights under U.S. law is an essential resource for legal aid programs, community groups, and social service agencies across the country.

National Network for Immigrant and Refugee Rights (NNIRR)
310 8th Street, Suite 303
Oakland, CA 94607
510-465-1984
http://www.nnirr.org
NNIRR is a national organization composed of local coalitions and immigrant, refugee, community, religious, civil rights, and labor organizations and activists. It serves as a forum to share information and analysis, to educate communities and the general public, and to develop and coordinate plans of action on important immigrant and refugee issues. NNIRR works to promote a just immigration and refugee policy in the United States and to defend and expand the rights of all immigrants and refugees, regardless of immigration status.

U.S. English, Inc.

1747 Pennsylvania Avenue NW, Suite 1050

Washington, DC 20006

202-833-0100

http://www.us-english.org

U.S. English is the nation's oldest, largest citizen action group dedicated to preserving the unifying role of the English language in the United States. Founded in 1983 by the late U.S. senator S. I. Hayakawa of California, an immigrant himself, U.S. English now has 1.8 million members nationwide. U.S. English believes that the lack of an assimilation policy for immigrants to the United States is rapidly changing the successful integration patterns of the past. U.S. English also believes that government policies and low expectations encourage Americans to learn the language of its immigrants, instead of the other way around.

FURTHER INFORMATION

BOOKS

Anderson, Lydia. *Immigration*. New York: Franklin Watts, 1981.
Although this book was published nearly three decades ago, it is a
must-read for serious students of the current immigration debate.
Anderson's book provides vital historical perspective for our modern
dilemma. Readers will find that immigration advocates and foes of
a generation ago debated and quarreled over the same issues that
confront us today: Should we set immigration limits? What do we do
about illegals? Is immigration a benefit or a burden? The question,
says the author, is simple. Can we continue to support large-scale
immigration without compromising the quality of life in the United
States? The answer, however, is far more complex.

Benton, Barbara. *Ellis Island: A Pictorial History*. New York: Facts on File
Publications, 1985.
This thoroughly researched book tells how a pile of landfill in New
York Harbor became the gateway to the United States for about twelve
million immigrants over a period of six decades. The book contains
more than one hundred historical photographs, political cartoons,
newspaper illustrations, and architectural drawings. Along with
the history of Ellis Island, the book provides firsthand accounts by
immigrants who endured long lines, long waits, fear of rejection, and
dehumanizing conditions. Benton also includes commentary on the
social and political controversies surrounding immigration a century
ago. Readers who wonder what might have awaited Great-Grandma
when she sailed for the United States will find this book highly
informative.

Berquist, James M. *Daily Life in Immigrant America: 1820–1870*. Westport,
CT: Greenwood Press, 2007.
This volume explores the experience of immigrants to the United
States in the mid-1800s. Berquist details where immigrants came from,
what their journeys were like, where they entered the United States,
and where they eventually settled. The author also examines life in
immigrant communities, particularly those areas of life unsettled
by the clash of cultures and adjustment to a new society. The book

highlights immigrant contributions to U.S. society and the battles fought by immigrants to gain wider acceptance in mainstream culture.

In America series. Minneapolis: Twenty-First Century Books, 2005–2006. This sixteen-book series offers historic and cultural information about a variety of groups that have come to the United States throughout its history. Maps, recipes, sidebars, mini-biographies, Web links, and other details flesh out this broad look at immigrant groups in the United States.

Karmiol, Sheri Metzger, ed. *Illegal Immigration.* Detroit: Greenhaven Press, 2007.
This book is part of Greenhaven's Introducing Issues with Opposing Viewpoints series. The book consists of three chapters, each posing a key question about immigration and U.S. society, immigration law, and the best way to solve the immigration problem. Each chapter presents a series of viewpoints written by pundits, experts, scholars, or politicians. Questions to consider preface each essay. Each ends with an evaluation and more questions to ponder. This book is a great tool to stimulate discussion.

Miller, Debra A., ed. *Illegal Immigration.* Detroit: Greenhaven Press, 2007.
This title is part of Greenhaven's Current Controversies series. It presents a very diverse collection of sources representing all sides of the ongoing immigration debate. The book consists of four chapters, each posing a major question, such as Is Illegal Immigration a Serious Problem for the United States? Each chapter then provides in-depth pro/con arguments from sources such as the Associated Press, the American Immigration Law Foundation, and President George W. Bush. This publication takes a thorough and balanced look at the social, political, and economic controversies swirling around modern U.S. immigration.

Wepman, Dennis. *Immigration.* New York: Facts on File, 2007.
This book examines the history of immigrants in the United States from colonial times through the early twenty-first century. It presents the voices of immigrants as well as data on U.S. immigration. Each chapter begins by describing the experiences of immigrants as well as the reactions of U.S. religious and political leaders, social workers, and more. A chronology of events highlights important dates in the

history of immigration. The book also offers biographies of more than one hundred important individuals, a collection of primary source documents, a glossary, maps, graphs, and tables.

FILMS

Golden Venture. DVD. New York: Hillcrest Films, 2006.
This documentary follows the ill-fated 1993 voyage of a freighter smuggling 286 Chinese immigrants into the United States. The immigrants had each paid at least thirty thousand dollars to the smugglers, hoping they would arrive in the United States unnoticed. The ship ran aground in a storm just 300 yards (274 m) off the coast of New York City, spilling its human cargo into the Atlantic Ocean. Ten of the immigrants drowned, and the crash injured sixteen. U.S. officials arrested the rest of the immigrants as they made their way to shore. The incident set off a firestorm of debate over whether the passengers qualified for political asylum.

In America. DVD. Los Angeles: Fox Searchlight, 2002.
This is the story of a modern Irish family trying to shake off their nightmares and realize their dreams in the United States. They cross the Canadian border and settle in a New York City slum. There they struggle to make a living, make a home, and cope with the tragedy they've endured. They don't find wealth and success, but they do find friendship and peace. The film's writer and director based the story on his own life experiences.

Sweet Land. DVD. Los Angeles: Twentieth Century Fox, 2005.
Inge, a young German mail-order bride, arrives in Minnesota in 1920 to marry Olaf, a young Norwegian farmer. But World War I has just ended, and Americans are suspicious of Germans. Inge also lacks official immigration papers. Local officials forbid Inge and Olaf to marry. Alone and adrift, Inge moves in with the large family of Olaf's friend and neighbor. There she learns the English language, American ways, and independence. Inge and Olaf slowly get to know each other, and eventually they fall in love. Still unable to marry, they live together openly, despite the scorn of their neighbors and the local minister's disapproval. But when Olaf takes a stand to protect his friend's farm from foreclosure, the community unites around the young couple.

Under the Same Moon. DVD. Los Angeles: Fox Searchlight, 2008.
This film tells the parallel stories of nine-year-old Carlitos and his mother, Rosario. Hoping to give her son a better life, Rosario works illegally in the United States while her mother cares for Carlitos back in Mexico. When Carlitos's grandmother dies, leaving him alone, he sets off to find his mother. Meanwhile, Rosario tries desperately to reunite with her son. Along the way, both face challenges but never lose hope that they will be together again. The film's website (http://www.foxsearchlight.com/underthesamemoon) offers links to organizations that help reunite separated immigrant families.

The Visitor. DVD. Troy, MI: Anchor Bay Entertainment, 2008.
In this drama, Walter, a Connecticut college professor, discovers a pair of illegal aliens, Zainab and Tarek, victims of a real estate scam, living in his New York City apartment. After resolving the mix-up, Walter invites the couple to stay. An unlikely friendship develops. All is well until immigration agents arrest Tarek and threaten to deport him. As Walter tries in vain to help, he finds his life changing in surprising ways.

WEBSITES

American Immigration Law Foundation (AILF)
http://www.ailf.org
The AILF formed in 1987 to increase public understanding of immigration law and policy and the value of immigration to U.S. society. Its website includes six program areas: Legal Action Center, Immigration Policy Center, Public Education, Exchange Visitor, Awards and Events, and Curriculum Center.

Border Stories: A Mosaic Documentary
http://www.borderstories.org
This website presents more than twenty short, focused documentary videos. The film crew travels the length of the U.S.–Mexico border in search of stories that portray the human face of this region. The site also invites visitors to interact with one another and the project's participants by discussing the subject matter on a companion blog.

Center for Immigration Studies (CIS)
http://www.cis.org
This nonpartisan, nonprofit research group claims to be devoted to
the analysis of the economic, social, demographic, and fiscal impact
of U.S. immigration. Founded in 1985, its mission is to expand public
knowledge and understanding about the need for an immigration
policy that gives priority to the broad national interest.

NPR: The Immigration Debate
http://www.npr.org/templates/story/story.php?storyId=5310549
This National Public Radio website presents news stories about possible
reforms to U.S. immigration policy and opinions about immigration from
political leaders, congresspeople, and religious leaders. The site also gives
voice to guest workers, Border Patrol agents, immigration protesters, and
other individuals actively involved in the debate. In addition to up-to-the-
minute news coverage, the site offers questions and answers concerning
immigration policy, illegal immigration, and the U.S.–Mexico border.

Public Agenda for Citizens Issue Guide: Immigration
http://www.publicagenda.org/citizen/issueguides/immigration
This website introduces the immigration debate by saying, "Americans
have always been ambivalent about immigration, with realistic
concerns bumping into altruistic, even romantic notions." It offers a
wealth of information on immigration rates, reasons for admission,
origins of legal and illegal immigrants, destinations and occupations of
immigrants, immigrant education and poverty levels, and more.

Yearbook of Immigration Statistics
http://www.dhs.gov/ximgtn/statistics/publications/yearbook.shtm
The Office of Immigration Statistics within the Department of
Homeland Security develops, analyzes, and disseminates statistical
information on the effects of immigration in the United States. This
website offers the *Yearbook of Immigration Statistics* for current and
recent years. Each *Yearbook* provides detailed data on foreign nationals
who obtained lawful permanent residence; entered the United States
temporarily as tourists, students, or workers; applied for asylum or
refugee status; or became naturalized citizens during a given year.
The books also present data on immigration law enforcement actions,
including alien arrests, removals, and prosecutions.

INDEX

Adams, Guadalupe, 50
Alfaro, Victor Clark, 87
Alien Nation (Brimelow), 113, 126–127
American Federation of Labor (AFL), 32–33
Americanization, 7, 118–119
American Party (Know Nothings), 23, 24, 119
American Republican Party, 23
Americans for Legal Immigration, 108
anti-immigration movement, 32–33
Araujo, Rosario, 105
Arroyo, Amilcar, 65
assimilation, 7, 118–119
Austin, MN, 66–71

Barletta, Lou, 64–66
Bell, Brett, 103
Berrios, Pedro, 94–95
Bilbray, Brian, 51
Binational Center for Human Rights, 87
border enforcement, 49, 82–89
Brimelow, Peter, 113, 126–127
Brown-Waite, Ginny, 79
Bustamante, Salvador, 115

California, 8, 27–28, 39
Cambodian immigration, 37–38
Carter, Jimmy, 38
Castle Garden processing center, 20
Catholic Church, 129–130
Chertoff, Michael, 84
children, 93, 97
Chinese Exclusion Act of 1882, 29
Chinese immigration, 27–29
citizenship, 8, 9, 56–58
Cockrel, Ken, Jr., 74, 76
Cold War, 35–36

Cole, David, 118–119
Colorado, 76
Communism, 35–36
Contreras, Victor, 67
Crèvecoeur, Michel-Guillaume-Jean de, 18
crime, 113–115
cultural diversity, 7, 117–119

deportation, 42, 48, 50, 93, 94–95, 96
Detroit, MI, 74, 76–77
Displaced Persons Acts of 1948, 35
Dunlap, John, 17

economy and immigration: jobs, 8, 104–108; positive impact, 71; welfare, 109–113
education issues, 108–109
Ellis Island immigration center, 30, 31
El Paso, TX, 88–89
employment issues, 8
English-language debate, 120–125
ethnic ghettos, 21
European immigration: 1800–1890, 19–27; 1890–1920, 30–33; colonial era, 5–7, 14–17

Federation for American Immigration Reform (FAIR), 110
Fourteenth Amendment, 8, 9, 60–61
Franklin, Benjamin, 7
French immigration and exploration, 15
future projections, immigration, 7

Gallegly, Elton, 42
German immigration, 25, 26–27
Gompers, Samuel, 32–33
Great Britain, 6, 15–17, 27
Great Depression, 34
Green, Gary, 70, 71

green card, 55
Gutierrez, Carlos, 53, 54
Guzman, Amilcar, 104

Haidara, Muhamed, 117
Harrison, Pricey, 109
Hart-Celler Act, 37
hate crimes, 122–123
Haya, 73
Hazelton, PA, 64–66
health care, 60, 71–72

illegal immigration, 7, 58–61; amnesty, 47, 50–51; employer punishment, 92. *See also* immigration laws
Illegal Immigration Reform and Immigrant Responsibility Act (IIRIRA), 41, 44–45
immigration, historic: 1800–1890, 19–30; 1890–1920, 30–33; 1920–1960, 33–36; 1960–1980, 36–38; 1980s, 38; colonial era, 5–7, 14–19; recent, 7, 58–61
immigration debate summary, 5–11
immigration laws: Chinese Exclusion Act of 1882, 29; Displaced Persons Acts of 1948, 35; Illegal Immigration Reform and Immigrant Responsibility Act (IIRIRA), 41, 44–45; Internal Security Act of 1950, 35; Johnson-Reed Act of 1924, 34; law enforcement, 73–79; local control of, 63–71, 97–101; McCarran-Walter Act, 35, 36; National Origins Act of 1929, 34; Personal Responsibility and Work Opportunity Reconciliation Act (PRWORA), 41–44, 110; Refugee Act, 38–39; sanctuary cities, 75–79; War Brides Act of 1945, 34–35
immigration reform efforts, 41–54

Immigration Restriction League, 33
Indiana, 72
Internal Security Act of 1950, 35
Irish immigration, 21–22, 24–25
issei, 29

Japanese immigration, 29–30
Jewish immigration, 30–31
Johnson, Lyndon, 37
Johnson-Reed Act of 1924, 34
Jurarez, Mexico, 88–89

Kennedy, John Fitzgerald, 24, 36–37, 131
Kennedy, Ted, 9, 43, 47, 50
Know Nothing Party. *See* American Party (Know Nothings)
Kosovo refugees, 73

language debate, 120–125
Laredo, TX, 82–84
Laurel, MS, 91–92
Lawful Permanent Resident card, 55. *See also* green card
legal immigration, 55–56
Louisiana Purchase, 19

Mandel, Michael, 9–10
Martinez, Mel, 48
Mayflower, 6
McCain, John, 47, 51
McCarran-Walter Act, 35, 36
McCollum, Bill, 60–61
meatpacking industry, 66–71, 90–92
Meltzer, Kim, 78
Mexico, 59, 82–89, 106–107
migrant workers, 99, 100
Minuteman Civil Defense Corps, 130
moral imperatives, 125–131
multiculturalism, 117–119

Napolitano, Janet, 82
national identity card, 8
National Immigration Law Center
(NILC), 75, 109
National Origins Act of 1929, 34
Native American Party, 23
Native Americans, 13–14
Nativist Party, 22–23
naturalization, 56–58
Navarrette, Ruben, 120, 121
Nebraska, 72
New Colossus, The (poem), 10
New Orleans, LA, 15
Newsom, Gavin, 74
New York, 20
nisei, 29–30
North American Free Trade Agreement
(NAFTA), 106

Oklahoma, 72, 97–100
old immigrants, 20
Opium Wars, 27
Ordooez, Oscar, 94–95

Patriot Act, 46
Pennsylvania, 7
Perry, IA, 91
Perry, Rick, 86
Personal Responsibility and Work
Opportunity Reconciliation Act
(PRWORA), 41–44, 110
Pilgrims, 6
pogroms, 30–31
Postville, IA, 91
Powell, Colin, 131–132
preference quotas, 37
prejudice, 21
pro-immigration movement, 9, 131–133
Public Policy Institute of California
(PPIC), 114

Quebec, Canada, 15

racial intermarriage, 28
racial profiling, 93
racism, 119–120
railroads, building, 28
refugees, 35, 37–39, 44, 54, 73
Reid, Harry, 52
Revolutionary War, 6, 17
Reyes, Raul, 70, 93, 96
Rhenish Palatinate, 7
Rios, Freddy, 109
Roberts, Pat, 43
Rodriguez, Gino, 83–84, 85
Roosevelt, Theodore, 29, 33

Saint Louis, MO, 15
Salazar, Ken, 120
sanctuary cities, 75–79
San Diego, CA, 15, 87–88
Santa Fe, NM, 15
September 11, 2001 (terrorist attacks),
45–46, 54
Simon, Paul, 43
slave trade, 15–16
Smith, Lamar, 42–43
social services. *See* welfare
South Carolina, 108
Spanish immigration and exploration,
15
Spinelli, Eva, 125
Statue of Liberty, 10, 11, 30
Strengthening Our Lives, 115

Texas, 84–86
Texas Border Coalition, 86
Toonkel, Rob, 124
Tulsa, OK, 98

United Kingdom. *See* Great Britain

USA PATRIOT Act, 46
U.S. Bureau of Labor Statistics, 104
U.S. Citizenship and Immigration
   Services (USCIS), 7, 54, 56
U.S. Customs and Border Protection
   (CBP), 55
U.S. Department of Homeland Security
   (DHS), 7, 54–55, 84, 96
U.S. Immigration and Customs
   Enforcement (ICE), 55, 59, 74, 78,
   79, 89–93, 96, 108. *See also* border
   enforcement; workplace raids
U.S. population demographics, 39, 103,
   117

Vietnamese refugees, 37–38
Voting Rights Act of 1965, 124

War Brides Act of 1945, 34–35
welfare, 8, 109–113
Wilson, Pete, 8
workplace raids, 89–97
World Trade Center attacks, 45–46
World War II, 34–35

xenophobia, 119–120

Zavala, José, 105

PHOTO ACKNOWLEDGMENTS

The images in this book are used with the permission of: AP Photo/El Paso Times, Victor Calzada, pp. 3, 58; © Hill Street Studios/Harmik Nazarian/Blend Images/Getty Images, pp. 4–5; © Three Lions/Hulton Archive/Getty Images, p. 6; © Spencer Platt/ Getty Images, pp. 8, 45; © Robert Deutsch/USA TODAY, pp. 11, 62–63, 118, 131; © Don Emmert/AFP/Getty Images, pp. 12–13; William R. Iseminger, Cahokia Mounds State Historic Site, p. 14; Library of Congress, pp. 16 (LC-DIG-ppmsca-05933), 22 (LC-USZ62-105528), 23 (LC-DIG-ppmsca-07575), 32 (LC-USZ62-61896); © Public Record Office/HIP/The Image Works, p. 17; © age fotostock/SuperStock, p. 19; © Huntington Library/SuperStock, p. 28; AP Photo, p. 31; © Keystone/Hulton Archive/Getty Images, p. 35; AP Photo/Houston Chronicle, Meg Loucks, pp. 40–41; © Dick Clintsman/Stone/ Getty Images, p. 42; © Chip Somodevilla/Getty Images, p. 47; © H. Darr Beiser/USA TODAY, p. 50; AP Photo/Khue Bui, p. 55; AP Photo/Johnny Hanson, p. 57; AP Photo/ Denis Poroy, p. 59; AP Photo/Michael Stravato, p. 60; Courtesy of Amilcar Arroyo, Editor of *El Mensajero,* p. 65; © Bill Alkofer/USA TODAY, pp. 67, 69; AP Photo/Charlie Riedel, p. 68; © David Paul Morris/Getty Images for Berk Communications, p. 74; AP Photo/Jeff Chiu, p. 75; © Sean Murphy/Stone/Getty Images, p. 78; © Eileen Blass/USA TODAY, p. 79; © Jack Gruber/USA TODAY, pp. 80–81, 86; © Tim Dillon/USA TODAY, pp. 82, 116–117; AP Photo/Joe Hermosa, p. 83; © Theresa Scarbrough/USA TODAY, p. 85; AP Photo/The Times-Republican, Ryan Brinks, p. 90; AP Photo/Jonathan D. Woods/The Gazette, p. 92; © Robert Hanashiro/USA TODAY, p. 93; © Sarah Leen/ National Geographic/Getty Images, p. 99; © Krystal Kinnunen-Harris/USA TODAY, pp. 102–103; © Chris Hawley/USA TODAY, p. 105; © Mike Mergen/USA TODAY, pp. 110, 132; AP Photo/Ross D. Franklin, p. 114; AP Photo/Minnesota Public Radio, Laura McCullum, p. 124; AP Photo/Rick Maiman, p. 125; © James Cox/USA TODAY, p. 127; AP Photo/Rodrigo Abd, p. 129; AP Photo/Khampha Bouaphanh, p. 130.

Front Cover: © Karen Bleier/AFP/Getty Images.

ABOUT THE AUTHOR

Robert Morrow is a retired news journalist who has authored numerous short stories and poems for children. His adult work includes a college-level textbook, a wide variety of articles, and an automotive journal. Morrow lives in northern Illinois, where he currently serves as submissions editor and marketing director for Boxing Day Books, a small independent publisher of high quality, special interest trade books.